PARAKEET RACES AND OTHER STORIES

PARAKEET RACES AND OTHER STORIES

a memoir

CINDY HALL RANII

authorHOUSE®

AuthorHouse™
1663 Liberty Drive
Bloomington, IN 47403
www.authorhouse.com
Phone: 1-800-839-8640

© 2012 by Cindy Hall Ranii. All rights reserved.

No part of this book may be reproduced, stored in a retrieval system, or transmitted by any means without the written permission of the author.

Published by AuthorHouse 05/30/2012

ISBN: 978-1-4685-4733-7 (sc)
ISBN: 978-1-4685-4732-0 (hc)
ISBN: 978-1-4685-4731-3 (e)

Library of Congress Control Number: 2012901761

Any people depicted in stock imagery provided by Thinkstock are models, and such images are being used for illustrative purposes only.
Certain stock imagery © Thinkstock.

This book is printed on acid-free paper.

Because of the dynamic nature of the Internet, any web addresses or links contained in this book may have changed since publication and may no longer be valid. The views expressed in this work are solely those of the author and do not necessarily reflect the views of the publisher, and the publisher hereby disclaims any responsibility for them.

CONTENTS

FOREWORD

This collection of stories began as a record of memories of our mother, Helen Margaret McGarvey Hall. "Moo," as we called her, died when she was thirty-nine years old, and for years it had been unsettling that I had very few memories of her. I thought that if I tapped into the "collective memory" of my five brothers and sisters, a more complete remembrance of her would emerge.

As I interviewed each of my siblings I was startled to realize that not one of them had more than a few memories of Moo. Following the interviews I studied the official documents that were developed at the time of her death as well as some notes I had taken many years back in talking with an aunt. From there I sought the insight of a physician who helped me to understand Moo's health and what went wrong. Conversations and correspondence with friends of the family and relatives representing three generations, helped to jog my memory and to give texture to some of the recollections.

Although my simple plan was to transcribe the notes from the interviews and compile them for my family, I found myself writing vignettes. As I wrote these stories I shared them with a small circle of people, and at their urging, I began posting them in a blog so that anyone interested could read them. The telling of stories of other lands and times evolved as my recollections criss-crossed decades and continents.

Many thanks go to Shelly James for her loving encouragement; to Rachael Worby for her urging me to "Put something down on paper;" to Diana Worby whose honest feedback and insights kept me moving forward; to Colleen Wilcox who patiently edited every page; to Lindsay Ranii for her generous gift of time and proofreading skill; to my early readers for their generous acceptance of my efforts; and to my wonderful family for sharing their memories with me. I'm not sure if we know Moo more clearly because of this work of collective memory, but it has brought me a deeper level of love and appreciation for each of my brothers and sisters and for us as "the Hall kids."

With love,
Cindy

Pasadena, California
October, 2011

A story not told is a story forgotten.

Anonymous

Part One

The Hall Kids, Dad, and Moo

THE LITTLE STORE

I don't know where Dad got his ideas of how to "keep us busy" after our mother died the Wednesday after Labor Day. School was going to start within a matter of days, so there couldn't have been too many idle hours for us kids. All six of us played tennis competitively, and pick-up games of all sports filled the driveway and backyard throughout the year. We used Dad's cardboard display boards for bases, had two sets of basketball hoops in the driveway, one for the big kids and one for the little kids, and I think that we were the only family in town that had a charge account at the local sporting goods store, Boege and Bean's. If we lost a baseball over the house, the offending hitter had to bike down to the store to get a new ball. That was easier than looking for it in the ivy. Over-the-house was an out. Over-the-line at the end of the long ranch house was a home run.

Years later I asked Dad how he came up with the ideas for the Little Store and the Lending Library. He didn't remember. He was surprised to think that they had been his ideas. He would say that honestly he didn't remember much of anything of those years. Dad had worked as a sales rep for a cosmetic firm. Pent up demand from the war years made cosmetics a boom industry, and he worked the territory from San Diego to Los Angeles. After a day of driving and calling on accounts he would go to his home office and do paper work for an hour or so. On the weekend he swept the patios, picked up 50 pounds of cubed crystal clear ice at the ice plant, got the car washed, and got a haircut. Sometimes he would play tennis or golf with us. Sundays he cooked pork roast with oven roasted potatoes, creamed style corn, and ambrosia salad made with canned fruit cocktail—the same menu every Sunday.

That first summer after our mother died, my three brothers were probably busy with baseball and tennis. There was plenty of time to fill for us girls with Dad at work and Moo gone. We had tried housekeepers and a nanny or two, but we six were way too much for any one person to handle. So, as a family we decided to take care of each other and the house and yard. We established Family Council. Dues were 50 cents a week with meetings on Sunday evenings. The boys laughed when it was suggested that Laury, the youngest at seven years old, be the president. But she did a good job. She actually called the meetings to order and built an agenda and conducted business. I don't know how she knew how to do all that. She just did.

We divvied up the work. Each kid had parts of the house to clean and we each had a night to cook. My night was Wednesday and I always made pounded-Swiss-steak baked with dried-onion soup mix and baked potatoes. Moo had taught me how to make baked potatoes. Sometimes when I came home from school she would be lying in bed. She would call to me to come back to the bedroom. I was the oldest girl, and she would ask me to help with dinner and to go into the kitchen and set the oven to 350 degrees. "Choose and wash eight russet potatoes. Then grease them with Crisco and put them on the skewered potato holder and put them in the oven." I would report back that the potatoes were in the oven. Sometimes she would ask me to get a special flat bottle out of the drawer where the placemats were kept and bring it to her. I was too young to realize what she was drinking or why. I would hand her the bottle. She would say thanks and tell me that I was a good, good girl.

Regarding cooking, after Moo's death, Debby and Laury were so young, seven and eight, that they shared a night to cook. Their weekly menu was boiled hotdogs and heated canned baked beans. They took turns using the little footstool to reach the stove.

Debby and Laury were very close, and together they started The Little Store. It was located in the playhouse, which was out by the backdoor. Built in 1950 when the original house was built, it was a replica of the main house with wooden shingles, paned glass and a real front door. Over the years we had used it for tea parties with dolls, a classroom for playing school, a secret hiding place for heavily armed spies when we were playing army, the way station for "parachuting" from the roof of the house to the roof of the playhouse to the grass while shouting Geronimo! There was no adult at home to tell us how dangerous this was, although the one time I tried it I had enough sense to know that I could have broken my neck and never did it again. To this day I have been cautious about taking physical risks.

The playhouse also served as a spillover storage area for Dad's samples and displays. The trunk of Dad's Buick was the main space for his wares: high-end cosmetics that he showed to well-dressed buyers in the department stores and drugstore chains of Southern California. When our friends would see the endless supply of lipsticks, powders, rouges, nail polish and perfumes in the playhouse they couldn't believe it. They were taken aback when we said they could have as many items as they wanted. It was the similar surprise that kids experienced when they saw our drawer full of candy bars in the kitchen and when we were able to charge purchases with the ice cream man or the Helm's Bakery truck man.

It was that first summer after Moo died that Dad told Debby and Laury that they could start a little store in the playhouse. First they had to clean it all out and then they could organize some shelves with some of Dad's samples, price them and sell them to family and friends and deliverymen. The girls were having great fun with the project. They used nail polish to label the shelves: L, M, B for little, medium and big. All the customers had to ask about those abbreviations. Things started flying off the shelves. The milkman couldn't believe that he could buy a perfume gift set for his wife for 50 cents. The dry cleaning man regularly purchased do-at-home permanent wave kits. Neighbors started to drop in to see if we were selling real goods at these prices. The cigar box, which served as a cash register in Debby and Laury's Little Store, was always full. By Christmas time all the kids were in on the act. We set up displays on the ping-pong table in the garage. Dad gave us some white satin material to drape over another table and showed us how to showcase items on different levels. Word started to spread. Our teachers stopped by to do their Christmas shopping. Mr. Gott, the 90-year-old toothless man who mowed the lawn, bought a bright red nail polish for his daughter. Soon after Christmas, Dad figured that The Little Store was becoming too public. The Company wouldn't be happy to find out about it, and it would need to be phased out.

Dad let me continue the Lending Library, but with only one customer, I let it fade away. Over the summer I had catalogued every book on the shelves of our study. I didn't catalogue the encyclopedias, because Dad said that we shouldn't rent out parts of a set. I didn't catalogue the children's books, because I thought that people should be able to borrow those for free. Each book in Cindy's Lending Library was represented on a three by five card and the cards were in a little metal gray file box with a flip-up lid that I thought was very nifty. I even had a date stamp that I changed every day. My plan was to stamp-in the checkout date and the date returned. I would charge five cents a day per book with a discount for three books or more. Most of the books, I realized, were from my mother's Book of the Month Club. A few of the books seemed well-worn, but for the most part it felt like they had only been opened to the frontispiece where Moo had signed her name, Helen Margaret Hall, although she usually she signed her name Mrs. Robert Hall. She must have liked to read, but I can't picture her with a book in her hand. Reading to oneself doesn't get much play.

QUILT GAME

Outsiders looking in on our large family saw the façade that my mother had created: six nice-looking, well-dressed, well-behaved children so close together that many assumed that some of us were twins. Moo had eight pregnancies in ten years and the toll that took on her would play out all too early; but she seemed to thrive on presenting her family to the world. We were the Hall kids, and we were her identity.

It was the Friday-night, public-face family that was Moo's dream. On Friday nights she and Dad would take us to the Snack Shop, a Coco's-type coffee shop. We would sit in one of the two booth locations that was large enough to seat eight, and the evening was always punctuated with people stopping by to congratulate our mom and dad on having such a lovely family. We all knew to smile and behave ourselves. As I recall, it was the only hour in the week in which there was no fussing or bickering.

We lived in Fullerton, and in the '50's it was still a small town in the midst of what would become sprawling Orange County, California. There were no chain stores, and many of the shopkeepers knew us or knew of us. When I would go to the drug store, sporting goods store or the grocery store, folks wouldn't call me Cindy but "one of the Hall kids." We all played tennis and rode our bikes around town. We were good students and "good citizens" and had that small town modicum of notoriety. We became even more notable after Moo died.

She had always dressed us all alike: the three boys, first in line of the six, in matching dress shirts and ironed pants and we three girls in matching dresses and bows in our pony tails. And the bows always matched the socks. Exact matches—ordered special from the department store if need be. For Easter pictures she dressed the boys in suits complete with hankies in the breast pockets, their hair slicked down with Brilliantine. We girls wore frilly dresses with stiff slips underneath. The outfits included basket-type purses with little bunnies inside, flowered hats, patent shoes and lace-edged socks. Photos were taken with the boys in the back row: Bobby, Mikey and Stevey and the girls in the front row: Cindy, Debby and Laury. This was not the era of T-shirts and jeans and tennis shoes.

As with any group of siblings there was fussing and fighting. If it wasn't Bobby against Mikey it was me against Debby or the boys against the girls—so many permutations were possible. The bickering was pervasive and no doubt wearing on our parents. My parents' bathroom was next to the bedroom I shared with my sisters. I remember one night when our mom was taking a bath and crying. She sounded in pain and deeply sad as she lamented to Dad that she didn't know how to handle "these kids" anymore. Her dream was of this family of *little* kids. She wasn't prepared for the reality that we would all grow up. Her drinking increased with each birthday, and she told our Aunt Virginia that she didn't ever want to be 40. Moo died soon after Bobby became a teenager and just before Mikey entered high school. She was 39.

Her death came without warning—at least to us kids. We were told that it was a heart attack, but it wasn't. In those days it wasn't acceptable to talk about the slow suicide of alcoholism or to encourage grieving or reflection. Her closet and dressing table were cleaned out right away; there weren't any pictures of her in the house. I hunted and hunted for photos that included her. There was one home movie shot by Uncle Bill that showed her—thin and wearing sunglasses. Memories were few. We didn't talk about her or her death and feared the use of the word "mother" at school. I was terrified that someone might mention her or her death. People later said, "We knew Helen was a social drinker, but we didn't realize that she had a real problem." We kids and Dad didn't grieve openly at all. If there was private crying it was just that—private and never discussed. But we could sure play a tough game of football, tenacious tennis or our all-out Quilt Game.

Quilt Game was one of those roughhousing, energy releasing games that we turned to after Moo passed away. Our house, 1010 Grandview, had a long hallway. It had a hardwood floor, and it was great fun to run and slide on stocking feet. The hallway connected the living room with our parent's bedroom and there were doors on either end. We invented endless varieties of races and games in the hallway: bowling with a real bowling ball and plastic pins, "walking on the walls" by placing one bare foot on each wall, and setting up a target range for Mikey's rubber-bullet machine gun. This was postwar America and playing army was part of any kid's repertoire.

Quilt Game was simple. Any-aged kid could play and any number of kids could join in. It was the perfect game for the rare days we couldn't play outside or when we wanted to initiate kids into the world of the Halls. One kid was "It," and we placed a beautiful, satin, mauve-colored quilt over his or her body. It was an oversized quilt so there was no light sneaking in from the floor. Fully covered, the "It" kid started at the opening to the living room and tried to traverse the 30 feet or so to the opening of our parent's room. The job of all the other kids was to stop "It." No other rules. You could jump on shoulders, tackle low, run full on with a body block or double up and have one kid kneel in front of "It" while another one would push "It" over the kneeling kid. One insidious strategy was to be very quiet and let "It" move cautiously down the hallway, gaining false confidence with every tentative step. All the others would be silently laughing and waiting for the group attack just at the last second.

You could really get roughed up playing Quilt Game, but you knew that you weren't going to break a leg or end up bleeding. When you were tackled the silky quilt muffled the blows. I liked being "It." I enjoyed the abandon of the game and had every confidence that I could make it to the end of the hallway. That wasn't always the case, but I always thought I could. Bobby, the oldest, was Quilt Game champion. We could neither slow him nor bring him down. "Plowing, cannot stop," was his motto. He is still tough—playing softball well into his late '60's. He always finds a way to get on base. I would still bet on him to make it to the end of any hallway if needed.

In my 20's, when I was dating my husband to be, we were being goofy one night with some grad school friends. I was telling the story of Quilt Game and suggested that we play. It would be fun. Jim hated sports and declined by saying that it sounded like a horrible game and he certainly didn't want to play. We cajoled him and he gave in. He chose to be "It.". We set the start and finish lines and covered Jim with an afghan blanket. Before the rest of us could coordinate our attack, Jim bolted down the apartment hallway, plowing through all of us and crashing me into and through a closet door. He got to the end of the hallway, took off the afghan and announced, "I told you I didn't want to play." I looked at Jim in a different way after Quilt Game. The "new kid" had passed the initiation.

Nana's House

Going down to Nana's house was always a treat. The house was actually a second floor apartment, which was perpetually in a bit of a mess. We entered the old building via a dark, interior set of stairs. The light at the bottom of the stairs never seemed to work, so it was a little scary until we hit the hallway. Stacks of "National Geographic" magazines and bags full of donations for the VA Hospital lined the walls.

Once inside we were comforted by Nana's collection of 280 pairs of salt and pepper shakers, a pegboard-wall full of kitchen utensils, and little signs with puzzling sayings such as "There's many a slip 'twixt the cup and the lip" and "Be sure mind is in gear before putting mouth into motion." There was, of course, the refrigerator. We knew that inside there would be a little Dixie cup full of cookie dough for each of us with our name on it. She spoiled us terribly. She would make sour-milk chocolate cake and homemade noodles. When she made angel food cake she would whip the egg whites by hand. We would watch the fat under her arm flap back and forth and laugh and laugh. "Oh, you kids!" she would say with the same intonation every time.

Nana's was a safe place and just two miles from our house. Grampy lived there, too, of course, but Nana was such a dominant personality that we just referred to the place as Nana's. We three girls would go there sometimes for short visits and even a sleepover now and again. Being there served as a respite from the bickering and fighting that was all too often the norm at home. Without our older brothers around we could watch what we wanted on TV, and we could let our guards down a bit without the threat of being teased about any little thing. So it didn't seem strange to me when we three girls were put in Nana's car that early September evening up at the Grandview house to go spend the night at her house. It did strike me as odd that our mother, Moo, was coming with us.

What I didn't know then was that things had come to a head. We all had gone to a Labor Day barbeque at Uncle Bill and Aunt Virginia's. Bill and Virginia had taken Dad aside and insisted, "Bob, you have a problem with Helen." Some other friends there also pressed the point. It was 1957. "Intervention" was hardly in our culture's vocabulary, but the message to Dad was being pushed firmly: "Helen's drinking is getting out of hand." She was having bottles of Sunnybrook delivered to the house from Charlie Hale's liquor store. On the rare times that Dad and Moo went out to eat she would drink on the way to the restaurant and have drinks for dinner. Dad no longer allowed her to go with him to company functions; she had become an embarrassment. The year before she died she ignored Dad's ban and drove the thirty miles to Los Angeles to join him at a fancy cosmetic industry trade show at the Biltmore Hotel. For some reason she had taken me with her that night. I remember his being angry with her and criticizing her for the gray suit she was wearing.

Dad wasn't one to take on problems openly. His style was to avoid issues until they simply could not be ignored. For how many years Moo struggled silently at home no one knows. It must have taken some convincing to have Dad tackle the issue of Moo's drinking and growing dysfunction. Going down to Nana's that night was the compromise that had been struck between my parents. Dad said that Moo had to go to a sanitarium to "dry out." Things could not go on the way they were. She had to go check-in somewhere.

I didn't realize she had a drinking problem, although Bobby and Mikey, the two oldest, were aware of it. Stevey had some hints, but we girls were too young to put the signs together. I was 10; Debby 8 and Laury 6. Somehow, Moo always managed to keep the family and house together. Everyday the beds were made with tightly tucked sheets; we were dressed impeccably with never a hand-me-down, and we girls wore ironed dresses with sashes and high quality, ribbon bows hand-tied around our pony tails. One by one she would seat us on the high stool off the kitchen. We could see ourselves in a facing mirror—sort of like a beauty shop. She would brush our long hair straight back into those ponytails and top off the look with the signature bows. Then off we would go to school.

Upon coming home we would often find Moo back in bed or on the couch in the playroom. We would all go play outside—whatever sport was in season. But somehow every night she managed to get dinner on the table. I don't think she ate much.

One day while Moo was in the kitchen fixing dinner, I was in the large family room playing the piano. My dad's mom, Grandma Hall, had bought it for me for $50. It was an old upright player piano and we all enjoyed pumping the pedals and playing the piano rolls. I didn't take lessons, but I was using a teach-yourself book to try to sight read a song. It didn't sound quite right. From the kitchen Moo said, "You need to play a B flat." I didn't know what that meant. I played it wrong again. "The black key," she said. "On that note, play the black key to the left of what you are playing." I hadn't known that she could play the piano. Actually, I didn't even know she had been listening to me play.

She managed to hold the household together. She had everything delivered: the laundry and dry-cleaning, groceries, household goods, milk, cigarettes (from Bullocks) and birthday presents. The owner and buyer from the local dress/gift shop "The Pillowry" would come up to the house twice a year to show our mom the upcoming season's children's clothes. By that Labor Day weekend in 1957 all of our school clothes had arrived via the very familiar brown UPS truck. We assumed that all families lived that way.

When Dad told Moo that she had to check into a sanitarium, she said that was impossible. She could not leave the children. She argued that the girls, especially, were too young to be away from her. The compromise was that she and we girls would go down to Nana's for a week or so. She would dry out there. If that didn't work, then she would go to a sanitarium. Moo told the boys that she was going to spend some time at Nana's. She just needed a break.

So we went to Nana's house that night. Debby and Laury slept on the convertible sofa in the front room. They giggled and chatted for a long time. They were only 15 months apart and, like twins, easily found harmony in each other's company. Moo and I slept in the guestroom.

In the night I heard her get up twice. Each time she walked almost noiselessly down the darkened hallway to the bathroom. I could hear her gagging—like dry heaves. This was not the first night I had heard those sounds. Each time she returned to bed that night I pretended to be asleep. Late into the night we both slept.

When I woke up I said 'morning to Moo. She didn't say anything. I waited a while and shook her just a little and again said good morning. She didn't wake up. I touched her shoulder, and she didn't feel right. Lying there for some time I listened for noises in the apartment. All I could hear were the sounds of Grampy at the dining room table having a cup of coffee and reading the paper. Nana, I remembered, had planned to take the girls with her to one of her babysitting jobs.

I got out of bed and told Grampy that something was wrong with Moo. He went into the bedroom while I stayed in the dining room. Grampy came out and told me to go downstairs in the garage to look for a flashlight. I knew that there was one in the living room on the reading table. Grampy had very poor vision, and there was always a flashlight at hand. I started to tell him that there was a flashlight right on the table, but I knew it made sense for me to go downstairs.

Once outside I opened the old double garage doors. The first thing I saw was the odd three-foot high wooden statue used to advertise Old Crow bourbon. The statue was of a crow dressed in a black and white tuxedo with a red vest. It wore a top hat and a monocle. That thing had always seemed creepy, and it used to scare me when we would play in the garage. It was a leftover from when Nana and Grampy owned a small grocery store in L.A. They once had a stylish, Beverly Hills type house, but over time their finances deteriorated and they had lost the store and the house. That's when they had moved to Fullerton.

I looked only briefly in the garage, but there was no flashlight.

When I arrived back upstairs Grampy was just getting off the phone. Soon Nana was there. She was bustling around the apartment emptying bottles of liquor down the toilet. She was telling Grampy to throw away the bottles. Someone, I don't remember who, drove me up to Uncle Bill and Aunt Virginia's house. Their neighbors were building a sunroom, and although it wasn't completely finished, we had used it on the day of the Labor Day barbeque. Debby and Laury were standing there in that under construction room, and when I arrived Bill and Virginia told us that Moo had died. Debby and Laury started crying and Aunt Virginia embraced them. Uncle Bill pulled me close to him. I remember feeling sort of numb in his arms. I don't remember crying.

We walked across the backyard, through the kitchen and into the living room. The three boys were sitting in the slightly darkened room. It was quiet. The boys already knew. Nana had called them up at the Grandview house. Dad was at work making sales calls in the L.A. area. The three boys were sitting outside in the sun. Mikey answered the phone. Nana said, "Your mother is dead; you kids killed her." Mikey shared the news with the other two. Someone picked up the boys and drove them to Bill and Virginia's house.

Sitting there in Bill and Virginia's living room we six kids looked at each other. From the kitchen we could hear someone on the phone trying to contact Dad. Debby sat on Aunt Virginia's lap in a rocking chair that didn't have any arms. Virginia was saying that it was OK to feel bad. Understandably, Debby asked, "Who's going to tie our bows?"

The Limo

None of the six of us remembers much about our mother's funeral or the burial. As happens, someone must have put together the details, which included a car coming to take all of us down to the funeral home the morning of the service. A long, black limousine came up the asphalt driveway at 1010 Grandview. We were all gathered in the garage, and it was exciting to get into such a spacious car. On every other occasion when we six kids and our parents had gone somewhere together we had squeezed into the 1950 Buick convertible. Debby and Laury would sit in what we called the "back-back" which we thought of as a third seat. In hindsight it was actually the little hammock-type space that held the convertible top when the top was down. Dad had moved to California in the 1930's from North Dakota, and he loved the sun. Dad's company, DuBarry Cosmetics, supplied him a car but Dad would pay extra for an upgrade to a convertible.

Taking us for a Sunday drive was something Dad would do now and again, and he would speed over a series of bumps on a nearby street, Malvern Ave., as we shouted the names of the planets . . . one named for each bump depending on the relative size of planet and bump. Another treat was to scream "Whee, Daddy and Moo!" as we held our hands in the air while speeding down a steep hill, Richman Ave., and shooting up the other side. On the day of the funeral we all rode down Richman Ave. in the limo, but the driver didn't speed up. I bet that all of my brothers and sisters, as did I, thought of the "Whee, Daddy and Moo" game, but this one time we were all quiet.

In the limo there was room for everyone. The seats were arranged in an L-shape and there was a jump seat that flipped down once the door was closed. We argued about who would sit on the jump seat. There were glass bottles on little shelves and Dad told us to leave them alone—they were for liquor. During the short ride Stevey, who was 12 at the time, requested that we not tell people that we kids had killed Moo. Dad said not to worry—that everyone would know that it was a heart attack and that she had died in her sleep. It was some ten years later that we learned that there had been no heart attack. Admittedly, "acute hepatic failure" would have been a difficult story to share with six kids from ages 6-15.

A day or two after Moo died I was standing alone in the garage looking down the driveway. There were lots of people inside and several times I was asked if I wanted something to eat. I knew Dad had left the house, but I didn't know where he had gone. The night before I had had a hard time sleeping. I was OK when I could hear Dad's voice, but when everything went quiet I was afraid something had happened to him. Twice I got out of bed on the pretense of needing a drink of water and had checked to see that he was all right. Finally I saw the Buick come up the driveway. Dad and Mikey got out of the car and Dad said that they had just gone to the mortuary to see Moo's body. The other two boys had not wanted to go and we three girls, all younger than the boys, had not been given the option. At the time it didn't make sense to me that I didn't get to go to see her.

When Dad died at age 88, I was living in Northern California. My youngest sister Laury called with the news and said that they could make arrangements for Dad's body to be held for my viewing before the cremation. I was grateful to her for that, and my son Anthony and I went to say our final goodbyes. It was the same mortuary, but it seemed like a sunnier, everyday place.

At Moo's funeral we kids and Dad had been seated in an alcove to the side of the area that displayed the flowers and, I assume, the casket. In front of our area was a dark scrim from floor to ceiling. We could see out, but I don't think that anyone could see in. Driving away from the funeral home there was fussing about who would sit where. Dad barked at us, which was rare, and said "You kids didn't last too long. Couldn't you at least wait to start fussing until we get home?"

Although I don't remember the graveside scene at all, I know where she was buried . . . alongside a row of fragrant eucalyptus trees. The summer after she died I attended a Girl Scout day camp, and each day we would walk along a dirt path to get from the campsite to the ceremonial gathering area. The path was lined with eucalyptus trees and I realized where we were. I was pretty quiet that week. I wanted to have a fun time at the camp and can remember consciously trying to be cheerful. Dad said it would be fun and "good for me." But there was a sullenness that would set in that would be hard to shake.

Later on in high school I had been invited to attend the junior prom. Dad's second wife, Sallie, had helped me to rent a pink, strapless gown and I had an appointment to have my hair done in an up-do. At school, Sunny Hills High School, friends talked excitedly about renting a limo and figuring out how much each couple would have to contribute to the cost. I told them that a limo might be a lot of fun, but I would really prefer going in our own cars.

1010 Grandview

Dad and Moo had the Grandview house built in 1950. For $2,500 they bought three-quarters of an acre on a hard-to-build-on slope in a newly developing area of Fullerton called Golden Hills. The sixth and final child was to be born that same year, so the house needed to be designed to accommodate either four boys and two girls or three boys and three girls. Three and three was the outcome.

The architect, Jimmy Talcott, and landscape architect, Myrton Purkiss, were friends of the family; or maybe they became friends from the project. I don't know; and when I asked Dad years later he couldn't recall. For years Myrton was a regular visitor at the house and a close friend of our mother's. He would often stay for Sunday dinner and was noted in the family for being an expert at dressing our baked potatoes. He had a great laugh and everyone seemed cheered by his company. For some reason he didn't drive, and after Sunday dinners Dad would take him home. We kids would vie for the chance to ride along. His bungalow was off an alley and the backyard seemed wild and jungle-like. He was also a ceramicist, and for years seven of his signature plates hung above the fireplace, and each of us now has one displayed in our own home. Myrton had no wife or children; he lived with his friend Bob Bogard.

The 1010 N. Grandview Ave. house was built in a mid-century, ranch style with a shingled roof. It was reached by a steep asphalt driveway, which flattened out to the garage area. On the garage door you could see the impressions of thousands of tennis balls hit against it. There were four or five slats that ran horizontally along the wooden garage door and when the tennis balls hit one of those it would ricochet unpredictably. I think that is one reason all six of us became good retrievers and scramblers in our tennis games.

The long backyard stretched the length of the property, although a triangular piece of land was left untouched at the far end, beyond a fence. Dad said he didn't want another house reaching right on top of ours. After school, particularly after Moo died, there could be as many as 20 kids in the yard playing football or baseball or running Olympic events including high jump, long jump, hurdles and, of course, laps around the house. We would bicker over who would run the stopwatch. At 3:30 the Helms Bakery truck would come up the driveway and all of us, including our friends, would order whatever we wanted: donuts, cupcakes, bear claws. Dad had established charge accounts throughout town so that we could buy what we needed. We could even get cash at the Wilshire Market and charge ice cream with the Good Humor Man.

The hill in front of the house was landscaped with ivy, evergreens, palm trees and boulders from the nearby mountains. A switchback series of red-stained cement stairs terraced up to the front door. Each step was shallow and a bit hard for an adult to traverse. Moo had them designed so that they matched the size of children's feet. The front door was rarely used and the living room with its floor to ceiling windows and sliding glass door was also just a space to move through. The one home movie we have of those days shows each of the six of us walking out the front door and down the porch steps. One by one we laugh and ham for the camera. Dad then comes out and Moo, prodded by someone in the house, finally comes into view and quickly scoots down the stairs. She is in slacks, wearing dark glasses and she covers her face as she walks past the camera.

Near the Grandview back door area there was a three-foot high cement pool that Myrton and Dad had built. Dad and Moo wanted all of us to learn to swim and to have a place to cool off in the summer. The pool had no filter, so we used Clorox bleach to disinfect the water. We all fussed and grumbled when we had to empty the pool and scrub the walls which would tend toward mossy when left to sit for too long. The pool water emptied from a little drain hole that we would close up with a carved piece of raw potato and modeling clay. Moo had the kitchen designed so that she could look out the window above the sink and see all of us playing in the pool.

Many, many years later, without any warning, one side of the pool just crashed down and all the water poured out down the driveway. After that it was never repaired.

The house had an eat-in kitchen, which included a long, custom counter reminiscent of a coffee shop. Moo would clang a captain's bell that was by the backdoor when it was time to come in for dinner. All six of us kids would sit up at the "bar" on tall wooden stools with chair backs. We sat all in a row, by age, Bobby, Mikey, Stevey, Cindy, Debby, Laury, and Moo served us from the kitchen side. Beyond the counter, behind us, was the oversized playroom that was decorated in a Western/cowboy style, as was the boys' bedroom. The girls' bedroom featured chenille bedspreads and storybook dolls displayed on high shelves.

The playroom included wagon wheel chandeliers, polished plank flooring, and an elaborate revolving bar. It was a semicircle; and when it was closed it melded right into the wide wooden paneling. It could be swiveled open to reveal a full western-type "belly up to the bar" bar complete with brass railings and mirrored walls and shelves. The wooden surfaces were bright chartreuse. There was an inset area that one could enter from behind the bar where the "bartender" would stand. When Dad and Moo had parties there would be a tub of ice set up behind the bar. We little girls would enjoy martini olives, one on each finger.

Later, in the wild years, we kids managed to break the bar. Two or three of us would sit, knees to chins, on the bottom ledge, and several others would push the entire bar around and around. Sometimes we would make tickets and charge for rides. Part of the fun was going from the brightness of the playroom to the pitch-blackness of the backside of the bar. One day there might be a pinched-finger; another day some of the glass shelves would fall and break. Eventually the bar came off its axel. When Sallie, Dad's second wife, and her three girls moved in to "1010" the entire house was remodeled and the bar area became a media center.

The playroom also had two large closets, which were designed so that we kids could stand inside of them to reach all of the books and games that were shelved there. When other kids would visit they would say that we had everything. I assumed we were rich, but after Moo died we realized that we just lived as if we were rich. Dad would say that it was just as well that he had let her buy whatever she wanted.

The study at Grandview was set up just for us kids, too. There was a globe that lit up, desk space for each of us, dictionaries for each grade level, science books, atlases, two sets of encyclopedias and the annual encyclopedia update books that would come in the mail. When the 1957 volume arrived I looked through it to see if there was reference to our mother having died. On a bookshelf I found a portfolio of 8x10 glossies that Moo had commissioned to show off the house in its original condition. Absolutely everything had been purchased new: the silverware, the dishes, the furniture, the linens, and even a green-screened TV in a hardwood cabinet.

So Helen Margaret McGarvey from Wooster, Ohio, a self-admitted status seeker, had realized her dream of creating a beautiful and impressive home. The design of the house was featured in the Fullerton paper and in the Assistance League's Home and Garden Tour in 1951. It was billed as the "Children's Dream Home." Even the playhouse was staged with a new tea set and China dishes. Picture perfect.

Once Moo had created the Grandview house I don't know how she managed to take care of it. I know that she had everything delivered and she sent out a lot of laundry, but I don't recall anyone helping with the cleaning. I imagine her getting all six of us off to school, straightening up the house, making all the beds, doing some cleaning and then collapsing on the couch or bed, probably with a glass of lemonade with a shot of bourbon or two.

When Moo died Dad was faced not only with six kids but the house. Early hushed discussions included who would take which kids. Maybe Nana and Grampy would take care of the little girls. Aunt Anna May was willing to take me in, but she had five children of her own in a two-bedroom home in the Valley. The boys, family members were saying, were old enough to stay with Dad. But Dad quickly dismissed all of those ideas. "It will all work out," was a phrase we often heard him say, and later it would make us laugh to recall.

At first Dad hired a young "au pair" type to help out, but she was quickly overwhelmed. Next he hired an older woman, a Mrs. McCormick. After only a few months of these experiments Debby and Laury, ages 7 and 8, went back to Dad's home office off his bedroom. Famously within the family folklore they wanted to meet with Dad about something very important. He set aside his fountain pen with brown ink and his order forms and listened. The girls said, "Either Mrs. McCormick goes or we go."

So Dad convened a meeting of the Hall Family Council and we divvied up the work. The deal was that we would run the household ourselves. Each of us would have rooms to clean and other chores, and all work would have to be completed before anyone could play outside or go anywhere on Saturday mornings. Also, each of us would have a night to cook dinner with Debby and Laury sharing a night. Nana would cook on Tuesdays and Dad would cook on Sundays. We would take turns with the grocery shopping duties. Dad would sweep the patios. Mr. Gott would continue to do the lawns and Dad would take the laundry to Mrs. Kaufmehl's once a week. Allowance amounts were set.

Grandview was never again neat and tidy and clean, but as Dad put it, "Somehow we managed." Dad lived in the house for more than 50 years and in his 70's and 80's he lived there alone. As his health deteriorated, so did the condition of the house. One of the favorite moments in his day was to take a folding lawn chair out of the garage and sit in the last patch of sun that hit the property there on the cracking asphalt. Still tan and handsome, he would smoke a cigarette and look down the driveway.

When Dad's vision was failing and his step was no longer steady, he moved out of 1010 Grandview to a small assisted living home on Cornell Ave. The six of us worked together to have the house sold and we each gathered items that had special meaning for us. The house was sold "as is" to a family with two active and athletic teenagers. They added a pool and a billiards table and remodeled the living room to create a great room. I drive by the house when I am in Fullerton and looking up the steep driveway I grin when I see young people laughing and shooting hoops.

BACK TO SCHOOL

As always, school started the first Monday after Labor Day; the fact that Moo's funeral had been on Friday didn't change the calendar. It was a big school transition year for the family: Stevey was heading into junior high at Wilshire where seventh graders feared being initiated by being forced to drink Tabasco Sauce, and Mikey was heading into his first year at Fullerton High School, joining Bob (as a Sophomore no longer "Bobby"). Mikey was quite small for his age and an exceptional athlete. He was afraid he would be expected to play football. The "girls", Debby and Laury, and I were still at Golden Hill Elementary located just blocks from the Grandview house.

Dad and Moo had always been extremely supportive of our schooling, and doing well in our studies was an unspoken expectation. Moo made great efforts to voice appreciation to our teachers with notes written on beautiful, monogrammed stationery. Lavish gifts at Christmas time were quite the tradition. Every December a large box, brimming with elaborately wrapped gifts was brought to each school office for distribution to teachers, the principal, office staff and custodians. The presents were typically sets of cosmetics from Dad's company, DuBarry/Richard Hudnut. Dad was a salesman in this thriving postwar company and samples were plentiful. There were perfumes "Oh La La," "Seven Winds," "New Horizons," and "Danger," elaborate atomizers, "Cloudsilk" bath powders, lipsticks with names like "Royal Red" and "Primitive," art deco compacts with rouge or pressed powder, and powder puffs of white and pink. For the gentlemen there was "Three Flowers Brilliantine," shaving talc, and colognes.

Everyone at the schools knew Mrs. Hall and not only for her generous thank you's. We children were her life, and a slightly derogatory comment on a report card or a less than enthusiastic remark at an Open House would bring out the bear. Looking over old report cards you can see that our parents always took great care to respond to each teacher's comments. Sometimes Moo's handwriting was very steady and elegant. Sometimes her writing was more erratic and almost messy, just shy of out of control. Sometimes Dad wrote the comment or more rarely, just signed the card. His signature, "Robert L. Hall," was always made with the same strong strokes . . . with a fountain pen and brown ink. Her signature was always "Mrs. Robert Hall," as was the self-deprecating fashion of the day.

The oldest, Bobby, Robert Leslie Hall, Jr., was a stand out in every way: academics, citizenship, leadership, and sports, especially baseball. In the fifth grade Bobby's teacher was a Mr. Troeller. Bobby received excellent marks in every category, but in the comments section Mr. Troeller wrote that Bobby had missed some left-right commands in drills in PE. I don't know why Mr. Troeller was having the kids do close order marching in PE. Maybe he was a vet.

Our mother had written back to Mr. Troeller via the report card that she was "amazed" that fifth graders are receiving instructions in anything but simple physical education and more "amazed" that they are expected to "obey commands." Months later in the year-end comments she again mentioned the inappropriateness of students having to take orders.

Later, when graduating from Wilshire Junior High School, Bobby was expected to receive the top student award, the Rotary Award. Everyone was so certain of that outcome that after the third and second place awards had been announced, the other students in his aisle started to move aside for Bobby to go to the stage to accept his first place trophy. When he was not named, it was a shock to everyone, and Moo made her displeasure known to the teachers and administrators in the school. My theory has always been that Moo had let herself be heard once too often in the school office, and that was why the principal did not give Bobby the award. No way to know for sure.

It was clear that Moo's fierce advocacy for all of us was part of our confidence. Going back to school without her was new territory. Returning to Fullerton High School, Bob sort of shut down. He still excelled at school, and sports but some natural fervor to be the cheerful leader and to reach out to girls had been squashed. He felt a lot of confusion, and anger towards Moo, "How could you do this to me? I need a mom."

Mikey had a hard time choking back his tears those early days at his new school, but he managed to hold it all in until he came home. Regarding the football practices he had feared, he had gone to the coach and said, "I can't play football; my mother just died."

Starting junior high school Steve no longer feared the possible hazing. He feared those beginning of the school year forms he had to fill out in every class. He worried about what to write on those lines that said "Mother." Do you write, "Deceased?" What does that really mean? How do you spell it? Is it better to say "Passed Away?" How did she pass away, anyway? Do people think that we killed her? Had she been sick?

For me, I was afraid of the word "mother." I didn't know if my fifth grade teacher knew that Moo had died. Did the other kids know? What might they say? What would I say? Did she have a heart attack? If so why had Nana poured all the alcohol down the toilet? If we all hadn't fought and bickered so much she wouldn't have died. I can't say "Moo" died. Nobody calls her mom "Moo." Bobby had started calling her that when he was first talking. When Mikey came along and started calling her Mommy he insisted, "She's not your Mommy she's your Moo." The rest of us followed suit. Now that she's gone how should I refer to her? Should I say "My mom?" "My mother?"

Nobody said anything to me at school about Moo's death, but I would freeze whenever the teacher told the class to "take this home to your mom" or "have your mom sign this" or "be sure your mom comes to Open House." It was 1957.

Debby and Laury were in the second and third grades. Reading circles were the big challenge to them. It was the "Dick, Jane and Sally" era and every story had a mom, a dad, three kids, a dog and a cat. The girls would read ahead silently to figure out which sentences they would have to read out loud and feel relief if their segments would not include any reference to "mother."

Dad continued to advocate for us at school and he never missed a Back to School Night or an Open House or a baseball game or tennis match. He gave us dollar bills for "A's" and was a tough critic of our sports efforts. Looking for his approval in the stands is easy to recall.

The start of school thereafter always brought with it melancholy as well as excitement. When Jim and I had our own children and they started school we began a tradition of taking First Day of School Pictures. The kids would be in their fresh new clothes and shoes and we would insist that they pose for pictures on the front porch and then walk down the sidewalk and turn back smiling and waving. They got a kick out of it when they were little and objected appropriately when they were older. There were sullen "hurry up and take the picture" looks in the teenage years. Back to School had become a chance for a fresh beginning and a symbol of new opportunities and hope.

In the summer of 2005, I was stricken with Transverse Myelitis, a rare neuro-immunologic disorder that left me paralyzed from the chest down. I was a Superintendent of Schools in a high school district, and I was not able to make my opening day speech, which always included references to the First Day of School Pictures tradition. It was six a.m. and the rehab hospital was dark and quiet. My partner Shelly would visit me every morning before going to work, but someone was entering the room much earlier that day. I saw my son Anthony sneak into the room. He was in a suit and freshly pressed shirt and tie ready for the first day of school: he was an elementary school teacher. He said, "Morning, Mom! I came to take our First Day of School Picture." He leaned down and gave me a kiss and then held out the camera and snapped the picture of the two of us.

THE LEMONADE STAND

Dad was a commission salesman for DuBarry Cosmetics. We were very aware that he never missed a day of work, and we always knew that perfect attendance at school was expected of all of us. After our mother's death it was even more critical that we not miss school. Even if one of us was throwing up and feverish Dad would say that we would feel better if we got up and got dressed and went to school. Usually he was right. There was no adult at home, so school was where we needed to be. In the summer Dad entrusted us to take care of ourselves, keep busy, and "play outside!"

Dad embraced the raising of six kids with an outward calm. People around town marveled at how he did it, but he just said he focused on getting through one day at a time. On top of everything else, he did his best to rein in the household spending. Debt had built up due to my mother's expensive tastes, and, as he lamented, "A funeral is not cheap."

Sometimes I would do my homework in his office while he sat at his desk writing checks to pay the bills. He always seemed so organized and efficient at his desk. It was a heavy, substantial piece of furniture, and my youngest sister Laury still has it in her home. Dad would use a big check register with four large business-sized checks per page, and he always wrote with a fountain pen and brown ink. I loved to watch him re-fill the pen from the bottle and marveled at how he could do that without spilling a drop or staining his fingers. Neatly tearing off the perforated checks, he used a distinct, methodical rhythm.

During one of these bill-paying sessions he looked up and said that someone could make a very good living by sending out invoices for products or services that were never delivered. They could send the bills to people who have lots of bills to pay. The person writing out the checks each month would simply write a check for the minimum amount due and send it off just to move on to the next bill. "Right," I smiled as if I followed the point.

As a ten year old I didn't really understand money. I knew the words "charge it." I knew that a good report card brought with it a financial reward. I knew that Dad would give me a dollar if I were the first one to notice that he had just had a haircut, *and* I said, "You got a haircut; it looks good!" With a dollar I could go to the Saturday matinee at the Fox Fullerton, see a double feature and buy Jujubes and Junior Mints. I knew that when I had cooked dinner once a week, helped with the grocery shopping, and cleaned our girls' bedroom and bathroom on Saturday morning Dad would give me two dollars.

An early economics' lessons from Dad came when my two little sisters and I set up a lemonade stand at the corner of Grandview and Valley View. Dad was at work "making calls" and the six of us were at home. I didn't know how to make lemonade, and Kool Aid was something only other kids drank—but we did have orange juice in the refrigerator. Half gallon bottles of orange juice were delivered along with milk, chocolate milk, half and half, cream, sour cream, eggs and butter by the milkman. His name was Hap. He drove up the steep driveway every day, came right in the house and filled up the fridge. If something had soured, he would take it away. Each visit he would leave a new checklist order form on the door of the fridge, and any one of us could mark off what we wanted to order.

For our "lemonade stand" we three girls took a small table from the Playhouse, made a sign, "Orange Juice for Sale" and set various prices for different sized servings. It was great fun and I felt very organized and businesslike. We used paper cups for a small three-cent serving, tumblers for a five-cent serving, and tall glasses for a seven-cent serving. Other stands in the neighborhood had lemonade for 10 cents, so we knew that our prices were better than theirs. We also figured that since we lived on a cul-de-sac, we needed to set up our business on the corner to attract more traffic. We kept our cash in a series of Dixie cups, being careful not to mix the pennies, nickels, dimes and quarters. A couple of people stopped by and then a few more. "Customers!" Several of them looked puzzled. "This is real orange juice. Are you sure this is all it costs?"

Business was brisk; so it didn't take us long to sell out. We ordered more orange juice using the form on the refrigerator, and the milkman replenished our supply. We set up each of the next several days, and we even had people stop their cars to make purchases. I don't know if one of the neighbors told Dad about our business or if the Alta Dena Dairy bill finally tipped him off. He came home from work one day and asked me to come see him in his office.

He asked me if I knew how much we paid for orange juice from the milkman. I had never thought about that. He showed me one of the bills and had me do some simple arithmetic. When I looked up he said, "Doesn't pencil out, does it?"

He also volunteered one of those comments that took me many years to comprehend: "Besides, it isn't really safe for you little girls to be up on the corner all by yourselves."

Parakeet Races

Sports were clearly at the center of our activities at 1010 Grandview. Besides baseball, basketball, football, tennis (against the garage door), track, bowling (down the hallway), and ping-pong there was also croquet, badminton, darts and archery. Being the number four child with three older brothers it was always a challenge to keep up. To graduate from "hike the ball and go long" to really being involved in a play one had to be pretty good. By the sixth grade I was so skilled at ping-pong I always played left-handed when my friends came over—just to keep it friendly.

Among ourselves we always played to win. Even in early adulthood we would play sports in the backyard when we would gather from all corners of the world. Life would take us to Vietnam and Okinawa and India but it would also bring us back to the backyard. One year when I was in grad school and home on a vacation we all played a game of football. I had the ball on a running play when my oldest brother Bob tackled me in the legs. I fell down in considerable pain and was concerned that I had broken something. I actually ended up in the Emergency Room. I asked, "Why did you do that?" He answered, "You were going to score."

We managed to turn everything into a competition. Even the simplest of pastimes would be converted into a contest. Playing with a yo-yo? How long could we make it sleep? How many revolutions could we sustain Around the World? That wooden boxed labyrinth game? How many seconds did it take to maneuver the ball bearing through the maze? How many perfect games could we play in a row? A paddle ball toy? How many repetitions without stopping? Jump rope? How many repetitions in one minute? Pogo stick? How many jumps, of course? We also played the boxed version of "Beat the Clock," and we invented additional challenges when we had tried all the stunts.

On hot summer nights we would go out in the back yard and play Prison Break. It was our own version of hide and seek. We would all dress in dark clothes. The one person who was "It" had a flashlight and had to stay in the area of the little pool—our imagined prison guard post. The others would try to sneak up on the guard without being "killed" by the light. Our games were not without squabbles or injury. As Dad would say, "You kids are going to play until someone gets hurt."

With our mother Moo gone and Dad working long hours our unsupervised play often got out of hand. The boys used to set up the playroom like a boxing ring. It was complete with ropes and little stools and water bottles and boxing gloves. The family had a charge account at Boege and Bean Sporting Goods in downtown Fullerton, so we were never short of equipment. For the boxing I remember the boys as the trainers, and they would pit one of us girls against another. Sometimes we didn't want to box but they would make us punch and spar until they rang the bell.

So when Dad bought us each a parakeet it was inevitable that we would find some way to make it competitive. The jockeying began with which bird belonged to whom? Who would choose first? Then there was the naming. Who chose the best name? Debby amazingly recalls, more than 50 years later, the names of the parakeets: Pedro, Perry, Benjamin, Superbird, Happy Bird and Tweetie Bird. They lived in two tall cages in the playroom. Having the birds presented great opportunities to argue about who would feed them, who would clean the cages, whose bird made the biggest mess, whose bird knocked down the mirror, whose bird was the smartest, dumbest, prettiest or fastest.

Mikey's bird, Perry, was a different variety of parakeet from the others. That was great fodder for teasing him about being different. We often picked on Mikey and Debby for being small. The rest of us were more heartily built or "big boned" as our Nana always said. We spun elaborate tales to tell Debby that she was adopted, and we could be painfully convincing.

With no adult supervision during the day there were great opportunities to indulge in real life "The Cat in the Hat" escapades. Parakeet racing was one of those adventures. The playroom could be closed off from the dining room/kitchen area by an accordion door the width of the large room. I remember the door as brown leather to go with the Western décor of the room, an extravagance I can imagine my mother having selected. We would close off that accordion door, open the cages and urge the birds to venture out. We had competitions to see whose bird would come out first and which bird would fly to the ledge across the room first. My bird, Superbird, proved to be just the opposite of his namesake. He had some problem with one wing and always lagged behind.

One of us came up with the idea that if we flustered the birds in just the right way they would start to circle the room in a frenzy. Then we really had races going. Bobby, my oldest brother, would call the circling like lengths of a horse race. At the end of the races we were each responsible for capturing our own parakeet and setting it back in one of the two tall cages. Holding a post-race Superbird, I could feel his tiny heart pounding. I was afraid that he was going to die.

On one of those hot Prison Break nights it was too stifling to go to sleep. On such nights Dad would tell us that it wasn't really that hot. He would buy a block of ice from the ice plant downtown and place it in front of the fan in the attic crawl space. This, he told us, would cool off the house. None of us believed it made any difference, but it was a ritual among us to watch him try.

As for the birds, it was just too hot for them to be in the house. Dad, or someone, put the two cages of birds on the patio where we played ping-pong. The next morning we saw that the cages were knocked down and all the parakeets were gone. None of us said anything. Nobody voiced a word of blame towards Dad or to each other. Maybe it was the neighbor's cat. That's what cats do; they hunt birds.

In apparent retaliation, Stevey and two of his buddies captured a stray cat and put it under an orange crate. Using a backyard hose they were subjecting it to "water torture." My sisters and I yelled at them to let the cat go. Eventually they kicked over the box and freed the cat.

We didn't get replacement parakeets. The cages were put in the garage with the bikes and the rackets and the bats and the paddles and the mallets and the darts and the balls and the bows and arrows.

THE WILD YEARS

Looking back on the "wild years," it wasn't really that long a span. Moo died in 1957 and Dad remarried in 1963, so the period when we kids were home daily without adult supervision was pretty condensed.

With six kids, within eight years of each other, there were dozens of combinations that could go well or not. With our brood it often broke down into smaller units. Bobby and Mikey, the oldest ones, were known as "the boys;" Debby and Laury, the youngest ones, were known as the "the girls;" and Stevey and I, the ones in the middle, were known as Stevey and Cindy or "the Campbell Kids." That nickname, I think, came from our round faces and brown eyes and mischievous smiles. Stevey and I could giggle together for hours over the silliest play, like using food coloring to turn the water in the toilet blue or seeing how far an unraveled roll of toilet paper would reach throughout the house.

It felt like there was always some squabble. All of us clearly recall Dad's refrain of "Bicker, bicker, bicker . . . that's all you kids do." One of the most contentious combinations was Bobby versus Mikey. I don't even know what they would fight about, but in their teens it would get pretty physical. They would rail at each other out in the backyard and even throw punches. One day they were so out of control that Dad dragged them both into the house. Dad was usually unflappable and low key, so to hear him yelling at them was very unsettling. He took a knife from a drawer in the kitchen's chop block and he lay down in the center of the dining room. He held up the knife to the boys and shouted, "Kill me. Just kill me. You're doing it little by little with all your fighting, so just get it over with!" Everything went quiet.

I'm not proud to admit it, but the Debby-Cindy combination was another regular source of fussing and fighting. Debby could goad me into easy frustration, and I would tell her to stop taunting me. I would plead, "Just be quiet!" Then she would go to the classic threat: "I'll tell Dad!" I was a lot bigger than she was, and I would sit on her and pound her back to try to make her stop. She would also get me going by hollering, "You're not my mother!" I never consciously tried to fill the role of mother for my little sisters, but I guess aspects of it fell naturally to the oldest girl in the family.

Our household had a robust feeling of freedom and openness, but sometimes it felt that it might spin out of control. We managed to fight as easily over the extra pork chop at dinner as which space you landed on in "Go to the Head of the Class" or "Chutes and Ladders." When I read Lord of the Flies in high school, it didn't take much imagination for me to follow the story. I easily recognized the abandon of unsupervised kids, and our family dynamics certainly included power struggles, factions, cruelty, and a saving dose of civilizing instincts. At one of our weekly Family Council meetings Laury, the youngest, suggested that we should include "being nice to each other" as an agenda item. Faced with boo's and other loud objections Laury withdrew the item.

Little by little we managed to make quite a mess of the house our mother had so beautifully decorated. Stevey, for instance, had a little dog, named Rebel. Rebel was a mutt who was half dachshund and half something else. He was short-legged, shorthaired, brown, spotted, totally untrained and undisciplined. That little dog that Stevey *had* to have, ruined rugs, drapes, chairs, couches, shoes, socks, balls, and dolls. Debby and Laury had dozens of stuffed animals and every day when they came home from school they would discover that Rebel had managed to find and disintegrate yet another one of their beloved cuddly toys. Stevey never even housebroke Rebel, and the house lost its fresh, cared-for scent.

There were cats, too, that ran out of control. Shorty Homer Hall, the kitten we took in as a stray turned out to be a female. She had kittens as did her kittens and soon there were 18 cats living under the house. A macabre sortie with pillowcases is a shadowy memory. The boys helped Dad to throw the crying loads into the car; Dad drove off and the cats were gone.

There were also times when we would focus on elaborate playful inventions that involved all of us and sometimes, some of our friends. One such game was "Crank Calls". "Crank Calls" required two phone lines and multiple voices. In those days it was extremely uncommon for a household to have two phone lines, but Dad had the second line installed when we all started fighting over who used the phone for how long and how often. Dad's "solution" was to have two phone lines: one for his business (the "525-number") and one for all of us to work out among ourselves (the "526-number"). Later, when three stepsisters joined the family, a third line was the surface remedy to escalated phone-use warfare.

Our most daring crank call scheme required both phones. We would drag the long extension cords of the phones until they were close to each other near the linen closet off the hallway. The plan centered on Debby and her flare for the dramatic. Also, she had the youngest sounding voice, which was perfect for the set-up. She would dial a number using the "526" line, being careful to make the call to a number similar to our "525" number. Several of us provided background chatter to make it sound like she was calling from a busy pay phone.

When someone answered she would excitedly say, "Dad, can you pick me up at Disneyland?" The person at the other end would of course say, "Honey, I'm sorry but you must have the wrong number."

Debby would then go into her act that her friends had left her alone at Disneyland. She whimpered that she was at a payphone and needed to be picked up. She only had the one dime. The script for her was to try to convince the person on the other end to call our "525" number to say that Debby had called a wrong number and she needed to be retrieved from Disneyland. With Debby beginning to cry on the line, usually the person would agree to call "Mr. Hall" and pass on the message. Some good folks would go to great lengths to console Debby. One sweet woman even offered to come pick her up at Disneyland, which was about six miles away.

Of course we were all directing Debby and stifling giggles and even leaving the hallway temporarily to have a good laugh. When a Good Samaritan would call the "525" number to try to help, one of us would answer the phone and call "Dad" to the line. Bobby, 15, would usually play the Dad role, using the most mature voice he could muster. He would get on the line, listen to the explanation and then angrily say that he was tired of playing chauffeur to that bratty kid and that she could find her own way home! Then he would hang up or engage the caller in further psychological torture.

Those intense crank call schemes felt pretty dangerous. I worried that we might be investigated by the FBI or arrested by the Phone Company Police. I worried that Dad would get in trouble. Then what would happen to all of us? But the boys reassured us that it was no problem. "They can't trace us."

I don't know if Dad found out about the crank calls or not. If he did, I would guess he would have closed his eyes, shaken his head and said, "You kids." He had a pretty long fuse. I do remember one time when he marched us all into the garage for a group punishment. Maybe it was prompted by a particularly frustrating day of our fighting and feuding. Whatever the impetus was, he lined us up, by age, against the ping-pong table. He had us turn our backs to him and put our heads down on the table. Then, using a ping-pong paddle, he went down the row and gave us each a swat. The bigger the kid the bigger the swat. By the time he got to Laury, the youngest, the oldest ones were already laughing. I remember it as a comical scene, although Debby didn't think it was funny and cried for quite awhile.

We certainly put Dad through a lot, but his patience and steadiness and love for us all seemed to see him through. He lived a long life. When he died, at age 89, we all gathered after the memorial service at the cemetery. Dad's cremated remains were being buried right next to the plot where our mother had been buried almost 50 years before. After the last tribute had been voiced and the last of the dirt and grass had been replaced we six stood in a circle chatting. Then Steve said that he had recalled that these plots were closer to the eucalyptus trees. None of us visited our mother's burial place very often, but something felt "off." Following a bit of lifting of fake grass and some exploring, we realized they had buried Dad's remains in the wrong place.

One of us started laughing and then another and another. The family and friends gathered nearby must have wondered what those Hall kids found so funny. Although we all agreed that Laury, the titular head of our Family Council, would contact the mortuary director the next day and see that he set things right, I was comforted knowing that it didn't really matter.

He's There

When our mother Moo died, for Nana it was the second child that she had lost. Her youngest of five children, Jimmy, came down with strep throat when he was three years old, and without antibiotics, was unable to fight it off. Nana often talked about Jimmy, and a captivating photograph of him was placed prominently in her house. Jimmy had a beautiful face, framed with curly blonde hair. I sometimes hesitated to look at that picture; it was disconcerting to consider that a person that young could have died.

Nana once told me of how she had seen Jimmy in a church in Los Angeles. That was confusing, because I knew that he had died in Ohio before the family had moved to L.A. Nana explained that she had gone into a church . . . not the one she regularly attended. She started to sit down in a pew and a woman told her, "Don't sit there. A little boy is sitting there. He's there, right next to you. He is so beautiful with his blonde, curly hair."

I was seven or eight years old when Nana told me that story, and I didn't ask any questions . . . though I had many. Did Nana really think that Jimmy had come to visit her? How could that be possible? Did she ever talk to that woman again? Did she ever "see" Jimmy again? Once people are dead aren't they gone?

Nana did not believe in a firm demarcation between the life of the living and a hereafter. She went to psychics, and she was very concerned that we six kids had never been baptized. She went to the Episcopal Church and found it unsettling that Dad and Moo did not make church-going a part of our upbringing. After Moo died Nana argued with Dad that we all needed to be baptized. Otherwise, we would end up in Limbo and we would never be together with Moo. I looked up "Limbo" in my

"Dictionary for Young People," but it didn't sound like a place that kids deserved to go. We hadn't done anything wrong; but again, maybe it was our fault that Moo had died.

Nana was insistent about the baptism, and Dad acquiesced. One day there we were, all six of us, ages six to fifteen, standing at the font in St. Andrews Episcopal Church in Fullerton being blessed and welcomed into the church. I don't recall Dad being there.

Nana was the only one who talked to the six of us about our mother. No one else even mentioned her name, and there were no pictures of her in the house. All of her clothes and things had been rather quickly removed. But Nana would recollect Moo, her oldest child, who was now gone. "It is unnatural for a mother to lose a child," she would say. "It is not meant to work that way." I would think about that picture of Jimmy when she said that.

Sometimes Nana would ask, "Don't you ever think about your mother?" One day Nana told me that Moo wanted to know why we kids didn't talk to her . . . why we wouldn't see her. Moo would sometimes come to the foot of the bed, Nana said, and talk to her. She would ask how we kids were. How were we getting along? Nana told us that we *could* see Moo if we tried, but although I often thought of her I didn't really try to see her.

A dozen years later, in 1969, I was a senior at UC Berkeley. Unexpectedly I had a call that Nana was quite sick and hospitalized. I flew down to see her. During the short plane ride I reflected on how Nana and my sisters Debby and Laury had come to visit me several months earlier. It was the bright spot in my year. They had traveled by train and had a joyous trip. Their stay in Berkeley had been full of giggles and adventures and Nana wanting to have her picture taken with the hippies on Telegraph Avenue. Her twinkle had never been stronger, and one snapshot even showed lightness around her head that struck us as eerie but "just like Nana."

In her hospital bed she looked weak, but her bright, spirited self was there, too. We chatted easily, and she asked how I was doing and what I was going to do after graduation from college. I said that I was going to go to graduate school. There was scholarship money available, and I didn't know what work I wanted to do anyway. I told her that I couldn't decide between staying at Berkeley and going to the University of Pennsylvania. She said, "Go to Pennsylvania. He's there."

"What?"

"Go to Pennsylvania. You'll find him there." Then she smiled.

Nana died just weeks after that stay in the hospital.

Indecisive on what to do next in my life I figured that I might as well follow Nana's urging and go to the University of Pennsylvania. After a year in India and years of studying Indian philosophy and mysticism I was not one to discard Nana's possible premonition. So I left the tear gas, Peoples' Park, and hate-filled speech of Berkeley for Philadelphia. Soon after the start of the school year I went to a party thrown by Ruth Ruttenberg, whom I had met at Delhi University during my junior year in India. She was a City Planning graduate student who was also studying Tibetan. She introduced me to a nice-looking fellow City Planning major named Jim. We discovered that five years earlier, in 1964, we had been on the same ship together for 20 days when we had been American Field Service high school foreign exchange students traveling to Europe. Jim had spent the summer in Austria, and I had lived with a family in Finland.

This Jim Ranii, it turned out, was 100% Sicilian by heritage, and I asked him if it wasn't unusual for him to be so blonde and blue-eyed. He said that yes, everyone else in his family had an olive complexion and dark hair. In fact, when he was a little boy his mom would push him down the street in a stroller in their all Italian neighborhood and people would stop and comment on this little Italian boy, Jimmy, who had such a beautiful face framed with blonde, curly hair. Jimmy. I thought of Nana and smiled my own smile. A year later when Jim Ranii and I married, I recalled that other Jimmy and Nana's assurance that "He's there."

DAD

Dad, like his favorite singer, Perry Como, hailed from North Dakota. Born Robert Leslie Hall in Dickinson on May 28, 1916 he was the second of three sons of Pauline and Fred. Fred, whom we called Granddad, was a druggist, as pharmacists were known in those days. He and Grandma moved the family to nearby Halliday where they opened "Hall Drug."

As Dad would recall, the drugstore was a key gathering place in Halliday. It had a pot-bellied stove in the middle of the hardwood floor and a soda fountain, too. Part of Dad's chores included sweeping the floor, making malts and root beer floats and, as the story goes, filling the occasional prescription. The family did well, and even during the depression income from the store was steady. Old pictures usually show a shiny car and a very well-dressed family.

Up through eighth grade Dad and his brothers Jim and Bill went to a one-room schoolhouse in which each row represented a different grade. Dad jumped a couple of grades, or rows, and he had just turned 16 when he graduated from high school. He was the valedictorian at Halliday High School, Class of 1932. We used to tease him about that distinction, because there were only nine students in his class and one of them was his older brother.

The boys played a lot of basketball, particularly during the winter. Maybe it was those Midwestern winters that led Dad to jump at the chance to travel to California. It was the mid '30's. An aunt, who had moved to Long Beach, needed her car delivered to her from North Dakota. Dad had been driving since he was 12, and he and brother Jim didn't hesitate to hit the road.

Dad always showed great confidence that young people could take on big tasks. When I was about 13 Dad took Debby and Laury and me on a car trip to Zion National Park. On the long drive home Dad said he was sleepy and asked if I would drive so that he could take a short nap. Thinking he was kidding, I said, "Sure." He pulled over on the side of the freeway and had me scoot into the driver's seat. The only driving that I had ever done was on Dad's lap or on the Autopia cars at Disneyland, but I managed to drive on that 91 Freeway without incident. Fortunately, my little sisters didn't harass me. I think that they were just too scared.

So Dad and Jim drove to Long Beach, California. It wasn't long after that initial introduction to sunny California that Dad left North Dakota for good. His brothers and parents followed soon thereafter. Dad would find a job with McKesson Drug as a sales rep and marry Helen McGarvey, an émigré from Ohio. They had two sons and then Dad was drafted into the Army. After the war and a third son he returned to Los Angeles and went to work for Richard Hudnut/DuBarry Cosmetics. In a few years they moved to Fullerton, had three daughters, and built a house.

A short seven years after the Grandview House was built Dad found himself with six kids and no wife. He had always appreciated the sight of a beautiful woman and in so many ways it must have been hard for him to watch our mother Moo's health and good looks deteriorate. He was a vital man in his early 40's. He had Cary Grant good looks with his tanned skin, jet-black hair and aquiline nose. There was a family myth that there was "North Dakota Indian" in his blood, but there is no known genealogy to substantiate that.

As a cosmetics salesman Dad worked with beautiful, well-dressed, perfectly groomed women every day. As our mother Helen's drinking increased and her eating decreased, her looks and vigor inevitably suffered. Her hair thinned and skin toughened. Their sex life, so my Aunt Virginia once told me, had disappeared. Any energy Moo managed to muster went to us kids and the house.

It had to have been somewhat of a relief to Dad when Moo died. Sallie, his second wife, told me as much in a recent conversation. Moo had tried to hide her drinking and shunned any efforts at intervention. She would even wet the bed and Dad would ridicule her by placing a large sign on the mattress: "Lake Helen."

I am sure there were many women eager to give sympathy and love to this young, handsome widower. As part of his work as a cosmetics rep he once attended a radio taping in Hollywood. The guest star was Marilyn Monroe. She and Dad got to talking and he told her his situation. "I have always wanted children," she told him. "You are so very blessed." We used to joke that if he had played his cards right Marilyn Monroe could have been our stepmother.

Dad did remarry. In August of 1963 he married Sallie Handley, a young, gorgeous knockout of a woman who looked so much like Jane Russell that she sometimes gave autographs with that name. Sallie was the cosmetician at Longs Drug, one of Dad's accounts. We six Hall kids and Sallie's three girls were all in the wedding. Fittingly, since they both adored the sun, Dad and Sallie went to Hawaii on their honeymoon . . . returning with the tans of a lifetime.

On Sundays we would all go to Huntington Beach State Park and stay for six or seven hours. Despite fog or wind or freezing cold air Dad always thought it was a good beach day. "Just lie flat," he would say, "and let the wind go over you." He didn't go swimming or toss around a ball or build a fire. He just lay on a beach towel and soaked up the sun.

Given any spare moments at home he would sit on the back patio, his face raised to the sun. I imagine his being able to block out all his worries as he let the warmth envelop him. At the end of the day he would sit out on a simple aluminum folding chair on the cracking asphalt of the driveway. It was the least attractive spot on the property, but that was where he could catch the last of the day's sun.

Dad and Sallie eventually divorced and he faced other hurdles including a battle with depression after he retired, a broken back and arm, failing kidneys, macular degeneration and dementia. But he never lost his eye for a beautiful woman or his love affair with the sun.

When Dad was 80 my brothers and sisters and I arranged for someone to come help him out several days a week. Carol was an attractive woman some 25 years his junior. After meeting her he asked me to dust off his Sit-up Bench and locate his free weights in the garage.

Even in his very last days when he didn't know Bob from Mike or Steve, or Laury from Debby, or me from his sister (he didn't have a sister), his eyes would sparkle when one of the granddaughters would come to visit. "Now that's a pretty girl," he would say.

And when he sat in a wheelchair in his final days he would ask to sit in the sun.

Moo

Our mother, "Moo," was a McGarvey, a name that was well known in Fullerton, California, where we grew up. My Uncle Bill founded McGarvey-Clark Realty and he was "Mr. Fullerton," president of the Rotary and Chamber of Commerce, philanthropist and early promoter of Cal State Fullerton. We were pretty well known as the "Halls," but people were surprised to learn that we were also McGarveys.

Our grandmother, Lola Helen Donalson McGarvey, had also become a bit of a local legend. She, and Grampy had moved to Fullerton after a paint business they owned in Los Angeles failed. They lived in a less than elegant walk-up apartment and Nana, as we called her, always blamed Uncle Bill for not providing them with a house. Every time we drove by a certain property on the corner of Malvern and Highland, Nana would remind us, "That's the house I always wanted. Bill should have bought that for us; it's not like he couldn't afford it." Such were the early lessons in regret, lack of forgiveness, and bitterness.

Nana and Grampy were pretty broke, I think. Uncle Bill helped them with the rent and regularly brought cigarettes and whiskey for Grampy. "That's the last thing he needs," Nana would growl under her breath. Uncle Bill always called his dad "Pate," which visibly irritated Grampy and also irked Nana. "But it stands for 'pater'. It's Latin," Bill would say to make matters worse.

Grampy sat around the poorly lit apartment a lot. He would read, listen to music, and smoke cigarettes. Nana harped on him for drinking, so he tried not to do that when she was around. Sometimes he would pace. He often looked for work and occasionally found it . . . as a machine shop bookkeeper or an apartment manager.

Earlier, back in Ohio and Pennsylvania, Grampy had done very well as a representative for Alcoa Aluminum. He would tell us stories of train trips and big clients and a booming industry. When jobs became tight during the Depression one of the boss's sons was given Grampy's territory. Moving to California was the fresh start Grampy sought, but his entrepreneurial enterprises never quite clicked.

To make ends meet Nana babysat. She liked to say she was a Child Care Specialist, and she was great at it. She knew how to cook, clean, and nurture. Families competed for Nana's time. They felt loved and safe with Nana in their homes, and she had a somewhat mischievous twinkle in her blue eyes that gave people a lift. Raised one of fifteen children in western Pennsylvania she knew homemaking.

She had married William J. McGarvey, and together they had five children. Our mother, Helen Margaret McGarvey, was the oldest, born in Wooster, Ohio, on June 18, 1918. Four other children would follow: Lola, Bill, Ann, and Jimmy. The youngest died of strep throat when he was three years old.

Our mother, Helen, was smart, attractive, petite, very social and extremely competent. She easily excelled in school and won prizes in Rhetoric and Dramatic Interpretation . . . even at the state level. She played some piano and had sufficient interest and talent to move on to singing lessons. The center of friendship circles, she delighted in parties and dances and even had a debutante's "coming out party," complete with champagne, at the local social club. After high school graduation and one year of business college she and the family moved to California. For a time she worked as a telephone operator, a common occupation for women in the mid-thirties.

Besides her job, she went to the movies, dated, helped out at home, and worked as needed in the family business. When she had some free time she and her brother and sisters would join up with friends, sometimes going for a drive or stopping for drinks. Nana worried that Lola, the second of the children, drank too much, but she didn't voice any concern about Helen. Brother Bill thought that his parents favored Helen, who could do no wrong in their eyes.

Helen Margaret, as some called her, met our father, Bob Hall, through high school classmates of her sister Ann. Aunt Ann recalls that Helen would always make Bob wait when he came to pick her up for a date. Her clothes, her hair, her make-up . . . everything had to be just right. With bright brown eyes and slightly auburn hair she was always concerned with her looks. Bob, a dashing, meticulous dresser, was also equal to her quick wit and ambitiousness.

When she and Bob married, they, I would imagine *she*, chose a chic civil ceremony with matching suits cut from the same bolt of dark brown wool and pictures taken in front of the classic Union Station in Los Angeles. She wore brown and white spectator heels and her hair was stylishly waved. She and Bob had individual portraits taken at a photo studio, and no movie stars of the era looked more vigorously beautiful. It was pre-war L.A., and Helen McGarvey Hall was building her dream.

Helen wanted lots of kids and an impressive home and parties and jewelry and nice clothes. She wanted to laugh with friends and sparkle and feel accomplished and admired. As a start she and Bob rented a tiny but fashionable apartment. Soon they added a crib for baby Bobby in the kitchen. Pictures show that Bobby was probably the best dressed little one in the neighborhood wearing the finest clothes available including a miniature Army uniform as well as a Navy uniform and hats and shoes to match. Studio portraits and snapshots of him were plentiful.

As soon as Bobby started talking he called our mother "Moo" instead of Mama or Mommy. It was just easier to pronounce, probably, and, like other phonological reductions, it stuck. One by one, the rest of us Hall kids just called our mother Moo, and if we slipped and called her Mommy, Bobby would correct us: "She's not your Mommy; she's your Moo!"

Many, many years later, one of my grandsons, London, started calling me "Guy-ee" instead of the "Grammy" that the other grandkids had settled on. Now his little sister calls me "Guy-ee", too. Hearing the "Guy-ee" makes it easier to understand how we all settled into saying "Moo." I have always felt, however, that calling our mom "Moo," made it all the more difficult for us to talk about her after her death. The term adds a certain awkwardness.

When Bobby was only fifteen months old, Moo gave birth to Mikey; so there were two cribs in the kitchen of the tiny L.A. apartment. Dad was soon drafted into the Army and stationed as a clerk typist in Wyoming, but occasionally he could come home on leave. Stevey was born while Dad was still in the Army, leaving Moo home alone with three little ones. Moo had wanted a girl, not a third son, and as the family story is told, when the nurses first showed baby Stevey to our mother she told them: "Throw him out the window." She wanted things the way she wanted them. She soon became pregnant again, hoping for a girl, but she had a miscarriage.

She and Dad had been looking for a small town in which to raise their growing family and they selected Fullerton in Orange County. They bought a small but sharp-looking house on Wilshire Avenue near downtown Fullerton and just down the street from Ford Elementary School. Moo dressed the three boys all alike . . . everyday, even matching pajamas. They played in custom-made matching baseball uniforms, matching football uniforms, and matching cowboy outfits complete with chaps and holsters and toy guns and hats. Sometimes she would have matching shirts made for the boys *and* for Dad.

Moo became pregnant again and the doctor in Fullerton called for bed rest. Fortunately the pregnancy went full term, and I was born the oldest girl of the oldest girl. At Cottage Hospital, Moo demanded that she be released to go out to dinner; she wanted a steak at the Steak 'n Stein, her favorite restaurant. Neither the medical staff nor Dad could stop her. He drove her out to dinner on the condition that she would then go back to the hospital, the typical hospital maternity stay in those days being five or six days. I later wondered if it was really a steak she wanted or maybe just a whiskey sour.

Dad would recall that the years on Wilshire Avenue were good years. Our small house, however, was filling up and the yard, complete with wading pool and slobbering bulldog, was looking smaller with each child. I can only imagine, however, that Moo was restless to have a finer, larger home, one in which she could entertain . . . one, perhaps, that would impress. They started looking for a lot on which to build her dream, family home. Dad kept selling cosmetics by driving the freeways of the growing southland calling on Bullocks and Robinsons and I Magnin and the expanding chain of Sav-on Drugs. Keeping up with the burgeoning postwar demand for lipsticks and powders and perfume provided a comfortable living.

The move to Fullerton had also brought Moo a new circle of stimulating friends including artists, architects, landscape architects and well-moneyed real estate developers. There were the Muckenthalers, whose family mansion and estate was later given to the City of Fullerton for a cultural center. They had also built a beautiful modern home, complete with expansive pool area and maid's quarters in the Sunny Hills section of town. We would go there for swimming dates and the adults, wearing oversized sunglasses, would enjoy cocktails and conversation. The Talcotts, other family friends, had just built a spacious home in the Golden Hills area. Uncle Bill and Aunt Virginia were part of the circle, too. They bought and sold homes as they moved up the real estate "food chain."

Moo had another miscarriage. Then, Debby was conceived. Dad would tell us that she was the result of early headlines from the Dewey-Truman election of 1948. Dad and Moo had celebrated with cocktails when they learned that Republican Dewey had won the election. When they woke up, the news had been updated: Truman was President for his second term. But, as Dad would always add as postscript: "I can't imagine life without Debby, so it's just as well they got the headline wrong."

Dad and Moo chose the lot at 1010 Grandview: $2500 for three-quarters of an acre, in the Golden Hills area of Fullerton, near the brand new Golden Hill Elementary School. Moo worked with friend and architect Jimmy Talcott on the design and insisted on everything being top drawer. There was an oversized bedroom for the three boys, a slightly smaller one for the two girls, and a custom circular bar for entertaining in the large playroom. A more than ample play yard was integral as was a custom playhouse for Debby and me.

Then Moo was pregnant with number six. At the last minute she demanded that the bedrooms for the new house be redesigned to handle either another boy or another girl. When Laury was born the hospital staff sent in a priest to check in on our mother. She was insulted and barked that she wasn't a Catholic! Later, she and her friends would laugh about that exchange, and someone gave her a copy of the popular book "Cheaper by the Dozen," with the word "Half" added to the cover. That year, 1950, Moo's friend and ceramicist/artist Myrt Purkiss designed a New Years card for the family to send out. It showed a woodpecker that had just finished working on a tree which now said: Bobby, Mikey, Stevey, Cindy, Debby, Laury. The bird says, "Phew, this job gets harder every year!"

Moo continued to dress the boys all alike and we girls, as well. Sometimes she would have clothes custom made. One summer, maybe it was 1954, she had Hawaiian shirts made for the boys and Dad and matching sun suits made for all the girls. She didn't have an outfit made for herself.

Moo wore rhinestone sunglasses and smoked Benson and Hedges cigarettes purchased from the department store. The UPS truck brought them, packaged in a flat, metal case. At Christmas time she bought cigarettes wrapped in multi-colored papers. When she smoked, she used a cigarette holder decorated with rhinestones.

Our parents hosted parties . . . opening up the circular bar and moving the furniture to the sides of the room. Martinis were the drink of the day. Olives were like pretzels to us and I remember loving the music and the dancing. The garage was off the playroom, and Dad and Moo would set up a record player in the garage so that we kids and the children of the guests could have our own dance party. We played '45's and pretended like we knew how to do the swing. Sometimes we all would come in the house and do the Hokey Pokey with the grown-ups. I like to imagine great laughter and noise when we all did that dance together.

Five years before she died, Moo was able to show off her house and her well-dressed kids to the community in the annual Home and Garden Tour. Everything looked perfect and she received enthusiastic compliments throughout the day. After the last of the guests left she lay on the bed and asked, as she often did, if I would rub her back with rubbing alcohol. She said she was so tired and sore. Her back seemed fragile, her face drawn and hair thinning. She would lift up her head every few minutes to reach for her drink on the nightstand. The ice tinkled.

Several years later, as a ten year old, I would be helping her to fix dinner, taking directions from her as she lay on that same bed. Sometimes she would have me bring her a special bottle from the back of the linen closet, under the sheets and the blankets. Sometimes she would have me bring her a small bottle from the placemats' drawer in the kitchen.

Try as I might I can't remember really simple times with Moo . . . maybe sitting with a book, or singing songs together or watching TV or just snuggling. There must have been hugs and kisses and "I love you's," but I can't remember them. But I now see my grown kids enjoy those sweet moments with their own children: They take the time to read and sing and dance and snuggle; to play games and do puzzles; they say "I love you."

And when four-year-old grandson London calls me "Guy-ee," I just don't have it in me to correct his pronunciation. "Guy-ee!" he emphatically tells his sister, Berlin. "She's not your Grammy; she's your Guy-ee."

WHAT *DID* HAPPEN?

We all wanted to believe what we were told: our mother, Helen Margaret McGarvey Hall, had died in her sleep of a heart attack at age 39. "So young." "What a shame." "And Bob left with all those kids," people sympathized.

But right from the beginning there were whispered indications that we didn't know the whole story . . . or even the truth.

But if she didn't die of a heart attack, why were we being told that she did? Had somebody hurt her? Did she commit suicide? Why had Nana poured all the liquor down the toilet? Why didn't anyone talk about her? Was it because we called her "Moo?" Had we really killed her, as Nana claimed? If so, how did we do that?

At age ten I didn't voice any of those questions, but I would lie awake at night trying to figure it out. Maybe all of our fussing and fighting *had* somehow killed her. Maybe six kids were just too many kids. She was often upset that Bobby and Mikey, as teenagers, were getting beyond her control. Soon Stevey would be a teenager. Yes, perhaps it was the boys becoming teenagers that killed her. Some nights I considered going into the boys' bedroom with a tube of lipstick and writing "You killed her" on the mirror or on one of their arms so they couldn't miss the message.

On the other hand I had heard Moo say that she would never want to turn forty. Maybe she did something to herself. What was wrong with forty?

There were hints not long after the funeral that Nana was mad at Dad. What had *he* done? Why was Nana angry and saying "How could you have done that to her?" What does "Do you have someone else?" mean?

Coupled with these nighttime journeys of doubt were fears that something would happen to Dad. I fell into the pattern of feeling panic if I couldn't hear his voice when I was in bed. Debby and Laury and I shared a large bedroom and they would usually fall asleep before I did. I would lie awake in the quiet of our room and listen for the reassuring sound of Dad talking on the phone or moving around the kitchen. If I heard the garbage disposal running I would be terrified that his hand and arm were being caught. I would have to get up out of bed, on the pretense of needing a drink of water, to check to see that he was OK.

Of course I wasn't alone in worrying about Dad or trying to make sense of our mother's death. We each made youthful efforts to understand a calamity for which we had neither vocabulary nor concept. Little Debby, eight years old at the time, even developed the theory that Grampy, Moo's father, had put bad mayonnaise in Moo's sandwich the night she died. We were kids and we somehow knew that we didn't know the whole story.

There were never any family conversations about Moo's death, but as I grew old enough to ask questions a clearer picture began to develop. Yes, she had been a "social drinker," Dad would tell me. Yes, I thought it best that we just say it was a heart attack. No, it wasn't your kids' fault. She just died. Her body just gave out.

But had she committed suicide that night? As adults, each of the six of us wondered.

Some forty years after Moo's death my sister Debby requested a coroner's report. Copies of the microfilmed files weren't really that hard to obtain. Back they came in a manila envelope: Coroner's Investigation, Autopsy Record, Crime Laboratory Report, and Certificate of Death. Each report, hand typed, somewhat hard to decipher, complete with original typos and smudges telling the official story of an "unaccompanied" death. The content was stark with investigative and medical details.

With this report, we thought, would come clarity as to what really happened that night Helen went to sleep and never awoke.

Grampy had called the police that morning of September 4, 1957 when he found that his daughter, who had spent the night, did not wake up. She was cold and non-responsive. Two Fullerton Police Department officers Ray and Pearson, arrived at 109 S. Berkeley Ave. Yes, she was deceased. They found a bottle of non-prescriptive sleeping tablets on the dressing table at the left side of the bed. "What happened?" they asked.

Grampy spoke of how Helen had not been feeling well, and she had been up in the night vomiting. He added that she faced back problems from having been thrown from a car two years earlier, recurring headaches, vomiting spells for the last several years, a possible brain tumor evidenced by a seizure one year ago, and a "nervous condition." The Deputy Coroner contacted the family physician who added that he had not examined the deceased in years but that she was known to be a "silent drinker."

The autopsy showed no signs of any back injury, heart ailment or brain tumor.

There *had* been one seizure incident, however. It was one year prior to her death, during a trip to La Jolla for the boys' tennis tournament. Usually Moo didn't go to the tournaments, but for this trip my two younger sisters were left with Nana and the three boys and I drove with Dad and Moo to the regional championships. The three boys were in the back of the Buick and I was in the front, seated between my parents. All of a sudden Moo started to gag and sort of gurgle. She arched backward, and her head whipped from side to side. Her eyes were not right.

We were near the freeway exit to Scripps Medical Center. Dad pulled off the freeway and told me, "Take her teeth out. Take her teeth out!" I didn't know she had false teeth, but I did manage to remove them. We pulled up to Scripps and Dad started to get her out of the car. By then she had "come out of it" and insisted that she was fine. She would not go in the hospital. She was adamant. Only much later would I fully understand why.

We went on to the tournament. As Mikey played his match he worried about her and kept looking up to the stands to see if she was OK.

Had she been admitted to Scripps that day surely the doctors would have noticed what the autopsy revealed a short year later: a dangerously enlarged liver. They would have drawn blood and seen that even on a Saturday morning her blood alcohol level was elevated. They would have advised that taking large amounts of aspirin for back pain and migraines was not good for her stomach. They might have warned her that her blood work indicated malnourishment and that she needed to eat well. Her body, 110 pounds on a 5 foot 5 inch frame, was failing.

A year later the autopsy report would show that at the time of her death she had no food in her stomach at all. Her blood alcohol level was .093%, what would now be deemed legally drunk, although in 1957 the coroner's assessment was that "an insignificant level of alcohol is present." The report indicated there were no other drugs in her system, no overdose.

The autopsy report concluded that it was her liver that was the cause of death: Acute Hepatic Failure. As death neared that night there would have been internal bleeding; electrolytes would have been imbalanced; extreme acidosis would have set in; respiration would have become suppressed; circulation would have collapsed. Life simply stopped. Maybe what Dad had told me wasn't such a bad summary: "Her body just gave out."

Every few years I take a look at those Coroner's documents, and I even reviewed all of the findings recently with a friend, Dr. Shelby Dietrich. She is of my parent's generation, and she brought great insight into the "story" as she helped me interpret the reports.

Within the documents she saw a strong woman who, despite being severely debilitated by alcoholism and anorexia, managed to keep together a household and six children. "She was anesthetized with alcohol. She would have had no forewarning that she would die. She was so far gone with the cirrhosis that if it wasn't that night it would have been soon. She was in a downward spiral."

Dr. Dietrich went on to say that such a profoundly sad story was, unfortunately, not that uncommon, particularly in that era . . . women drinking alone, at home, taking care of their families but not themselves.

"There was nothing any of you could have done. Death was inevitable. Yes, her death was suicidal, but it took many, many years."

Mikey Cried

We didn't talk about our mother, Moo, or her death, and we never grieved openly. We sulked or feared or angered or wept singularly. There were no pictures of Moo displayed at home and we never collectively noted her birthday or the anniversary of her death. Aunt Anna May came to the house soon after Moo's death and cleaned out her clothes and belongings, although two or three fancy dresses were set aside for playing dress-up. Dad came to me one afternoon and gave me a pink jewelry box filled with rhinestone broaches, strings of pearls, dozens of earrings, a cocktail ring, and Moo's diamond engagement ring.

Everyday Moo had used a dressing table crowded with perfumes, makeup, jewelry, bobby-pins, brushes and combs. Until it was moved out of the house, I would sneak a quiet moment or two to sit at that dressing table and stare at the black and gold marred spots on the glass top where perfume had spilled. I can't recall ever looking up to see myself in the mirror. Everything seemed like a secret. I retrieved the matching bench and put it in my bedroom. It had a "secret" drawer with a dozen little compartments. My daughter Melina now has the little bench in her home, and her two kids use it as a piano bench. She tells them that it once belonged to their Grammy's mom.

When Moo died in 1957, most of us in the family tried to bury our feelings and act like nothing had happened. My oldest brother Bobby didn't cry much with Moo's death, but he hurt. He was often angry and withdrawn and felt cheated to not have a mom; he was just into his teens and needed her. One night not long after Moo died he lay in bed trying to make sense of the whole thing. He started to giggle and it built to a loud, extended laugh. He felt guilty about that tension-releasing laughing spell for decades, and he wondered how much his frequent fighting with

Mikey had put a strain on Moo. He had been aware of her drinking but had never worried that it might kill her.

Of the six of us Mikey was the one who let his tears express his grief. I never saw him cry, but he has told me that he would have a hard time getting through the day at high school. He would struggle to hold back the tears and then come home and sob—the grief arriving in waves. He didn't talk about Moo's death, but some nights he would set a place for her at the dinner table.

Mikey tried reading the Bible to make sense of her death, but that didn't help. He wanted her back. He wanted her back the way she had been years earlier, not the way she had become. She had seemed sick to him, skin and bones—debilitated and even pathetic. The night before she died Moo had grabbed Mikey intently and told him, "You are a good boy. This stuff that has gone on before isn't important. These things don't mean anything. You are a good boy." He wasn't sure what those "things" referred to, but he always knew that even though she wasn't around, he had her stamp of approval. Her last words to him have comforted him for a lifetime. Mike, extremely good looking and successful, has always seemed the most naturally balanced of us all, less anxious, more self-assured.

When Stevey found out that Moo died he was scared. He felt guilty and confused and wandered around the house feeling disconnected, insubstantial. He saw the mailman walking down the street delivering mail just as he had done the day before. "Wait. That can't be happening. My mother just died." He didn't cry.

Debby and Laury, my little sisters, were barely of school age, and they didn't understood what death was let alone why Moo was gone. No one helped them to understand what had happened.

I didn't cry when I discovered my mother unresponsive and cold. I didn't cry when I was told she was dead or when we went to the funeral. I didn't cry when we returned to school a few days later. But I found myself crying inconsolably years later when a kitten died, when I broke up with a boyfriend, and when my husband asked me what I wanted to do for Mother's Day.

My daughter Melina called me the other night and told me that her five-year old son London had been asking about his Granddad Scott's recent death. What does *dead* mean? he asks. Why couldn't they fix him? Where is Granddad now? Is he coming back? Will you die, too? Will I die? She answers his questions as well as anyone could, and gives him space and comfort as he copes with his confusion and loss. And she holds him as he cries.

1011 GRANDVIEW

Our childhood home at 1010 Grandview faced a long, narrow vacant lot perched on a sharply slanted bank. From atop our steep driveway we could clearly see that property across the street, its eucalyptus trees lining scrubland, which led to Hiltcher Park. Horseback riders used the lot as a cutoff from the park and it was our route to trails and streams and woods and mystery. I didn't play down there very often, but one of my older brothers, Steve, and his friends built elaborate forts and caves from which they battled imagined enemies. Occasionally realtors would bring young couples to look at the land, but it was too extreme a lot for anyone to build on. Our little slice of wild, hidden midst our suburban neighborhood, was safe.

But that all changed one day in the summer of 1959 when three cars parked across the street and stayed there for hours. One of the cars was a Cadillac and the other two were matching, small, odd-looking foreign made cars. What seemed like the next day surveyors ran string and chalk along the length of the property, and rumors began that a motel was going to be built. All of my brothers and sisters and I agreed that was outrageous. We objected to Dad who simply said that Zoning would not allow a motel to be built on our cul de sac. I didn't know who or what Zoning was, but I wasn't convinced that our vacant lot was safe.

Across the street the building activity continued. A foundation of red cement was poured just above the ridge of the lot, redwood walls were built, as was a driveway and what looked like a tiny garage, or maybe it was going to be the office for the motel. Prowling around at night with our flashlights we discovered that one whole side of the building was glass. One or two of the odd-looking little cars would appear now and again. We spied a man, a woman who seemed to be pregnant, and a couple of small kids. On a dare from my younger sisters, and to test our motel theory, I walked over to the building site and asked a carpenter what he was building. "A house," he answered simply.

The motel theory was extinguished. This was going to be a house, a strange house built by strange people who were placing a chain link fence across our entrance to Hiltcher Park. We might be able to sneak through the fence and make a break for it down the hill into the park, but the riders and their horses would be trapped. We told Dad about how the park was being cut off, that it wasn't right. Dad registered little concern. He said that the owners could do whatever they wanted to do with their private property.

As the construction continued we saw piles of sawdust develop. Debby and Laury, my little sisters, and I came up with the idea that if we could get some of that sawdust we could spread it around on our playroom floor and have a sock hop. Our mother had died two years earlier, so we were home alone throughout the summers and every day after school. We were free to come up with our own schemes for keeping ourselves busy, and the sock hop idea busied us for several days.

One hot summer's early evening after the workmen had left for the day, I snuck over to the building site and collected bags full of sawdust. I brought them home and hid them in the garage, worrying whether or not this was stealing. The sawdust would have been thrown away if I hadn't taken it. But it *was* private property, and I had trespassed. What was the penalty for trespassing? Would the police arrest a twelve-year-old or just scold her? Ethical considerations set aside, the next day we spread the sawdust all over the playroom and dining room and in our stocking feet we discovered that it did make for a great dance floor. When Dad came home from work he made us clean up the sawdust and said that we kids were "goofy". Then he went back to his office to write his day's sales orders. I was relieved that he didn't ask where we had found the sawdust.

As the house across the street took shape we sadly realized that there were no kids our age moving in. Also, there were no windows looking out onto the street, no real front door, no shingles on the roof, just red rocks, no house number, and no mailbox. To add to the strangeness there were two chimneys, one right next to the other, and somehow the two small odd-looking cars managed to disappear into the tiny garage. We theorized that there must be a turntable, like trains used, that moved one car aside to make room for the second one. The house was weird; the path to Hiltcher Park was blocked; and the people building the house were no doubt weird, too.

We abandoned our spying and went on to other projects. My next endeavor was selling greeting cards and stationery. Dad gave me one of his old briefcases, and I obtained a set of samples from a company that advertised in the comic books that we bought from the Wilshire Market. I knew I would make a lot of money. I set up my sample case as I had seen Dad do with his cosmetics. Order sheets, pens, pencils, receipt book and carbon paper were ready. My plan was to go to every house on the cul de sac and take orders for Christmas cards, all occasion cards and probably some personalized, embossed note cards, too. Those were more expensive, but they felt wonderful with the heaviness of the paper and raised letters. It was the same style of stationery that my mother had used to write notes to the teachers at school.

I set out at ten one morning, starting out on the right side of the street. Every one was very polite. "Oh, you must be one of the Hall girls." By the fifth house I was growing discouraged. By the eighth house I was choking back tears. No orders and only one house left, the weird house with no mailbox. Heading down the driveway I saw a round clay pot with mail in it hanging from an exterior beam of the garage. The mailman somehow had figured out that he should put the mail there. Looking for the front door, I focused on the plain brown door at the end of a long red cement pathway. Halfway down the walkway I considered going home, but I heard the sound of children playing inside. I took the final steps towards the door and rang the bell.

A lovely lady with a sweet, gentle smile opened the door and said hello as if she had been expecting me. Her light-brown hair was pulled back into a bun and two little kids with dark, curly hair, were running around behind her. I told her that my name was Cindy, I lived across the street, and I had some wonderful cards and stationery to show her. She said with great kindness that yes, she knew I lived across the street, but no, she was sorry that she didn't need any cards or stationery. Then she paused and smiled more broadly. "Why don't you come in for a minute? If you show me what you have in your case, I might find that I do need a little something." Walking into the house I saw a grand piano and a baby crawling under it on a red cement floor. There was a big crack in the cement running right under the piano. I wondered how a new house could have such a big crack in the floor.

The lady told me that her name was Meg and that she often saw all of us kids playing at the top of the driveway, riding our bikes, or heading off to school. She said that she often wanted to come say hello, to introduce herself, but she was usually just too overwhelmed. She invited me to sit down and she brought me a glass of water. The three little ones busied themselves and Meg had me show her every one of my samples. She placed a small order, patiently spelling her last name for me. And the address? 1011 Grandview. She said she didn't have any cash on hand, "Would C.O.D. be OK?" "Of course." We said good-bye and agreed that it was wonderful to finally meet such a close neighbor. She gave me a hug and stood at the door waving good-bye as I walked across the street and up the driveway.

Back in my bedroom I carefully completed my order form, tore off the carbon copy and prepared the envelope. I would ask Dad to include it with his outgoing mail. Deciding that door-to-door sales was not for me, I dismantled my sample case. As I lay in bed that night I was comforted to realize that I would need to go back to Meg's house at least one more time to deliver her order.

THE DRIVEWAYS

Not too long after I delivered those greeting cards to Meg, I was babysitting her four kids and pitching in on housework, too. I was twelve years old, and with my own mom gone, I was excited that such a loving lady across the street took an interest in me; and I was more than eager to do anything for her. It seemed that she needed some help.

Housework mystified her, she would admit. At times, the groceries from one shopping trip would still be on the counter when she brought in the next load. She was an artist and art educator, and every little thing was raw material for a potential art project. And there were animals that vied for her attention, too. One of the kids would adopt a snake or a raccoon mother would abandon babies that needed to be fed every two hours; and there were fish and turtles and hamsters and lizards.

Our house was sports and competition; her house was natural history, art and music. Classical music would play from reel to reel tapes; there was a grand piano in the front room and the older kids were studying violin and cello. Meg's husband, Al, an electrical engineer for an aerospace company, said that soon they would have their own string quartet. There was also Indian music and lectures on tape given by the "swami."

I loved Meg as a mom, a sister and a friend for some 46 years. For all of us Hall kids, knowing Meg made life lighter. When our grandmother Nana died, for instance, we all wore our stoic faces while Meg broke down in tears, although she had met Nana only a few times. Meg faced terrible losses in her life, but she still managed to bring love to all of us.

I worried sometimes about her health. Having lost my mom, who raised six kids, I feared that the stress of raising four kids and caring for a big house would take Meg, too. Often when I would come home from school I would see Meg at the top of her driveway. She would be methodically hosing it off, and the warmth of the Southern California sun would steam up from the asphalt. This "watering" of the driveway seemed to be a much-needed meditative break for Meg; I would watch her but not call out.

As Meg and I grew closer, she told me about herself, being an only child, her love of drawing, her studies at Pasadena City College, meeting Al on a blind date, going to Stanford and becoming a teacher. I learned about her mom and dad and their deaths, and slowly I opened up about my own experiences as the oldest girl in a family of six kids and about our mother and her death.

One day she asked me what my mother had looked like, and I showed her a picture. Meg gasped, "I have seen her. Some mornings, at the top of your driveway. She stands there and watches as you all head off for school on your bikes." Then Meg walked me up her driveway and across the street to mine. I didn't know what to make of what she had said.

I talked recently to one of Meg's daughters and she recollects that her mom had told her about the experience of seeing that vision of our mom at the top of the driveway. I retold the story to one of my sisters, Laury, and she shared that several years before Meg had passed away from ALS, she had asked Meg about "seeing our mom" at the top of our steep driveway. "No, I don't remember that," Meg had said. "But it makes for a great story."

THE EARRINGS

At one of our weekly Family Council Meetings Dad said that he would like to bring someone home for dinner for all of us to meet. She was very nice, he said. Her name was Sallie and he hoped that we would like her. He also expected that we would be on good behavior. He would cook the dinner, but he wanted us to pitch in and make the house look as neat and clean as possible.

Ever since our mother had died several years earlier, we were not aware of Dad doing any dating let alone being serious about someone. There had been, however, one trip down to the San Diego area. He had taken Debby and Laury and me with him and left the three boys at home. They were all in their mid-teens. Dad introduced us to this lady, whose name I don't remember, and we actually all stayed the night. It was really odd. She was sort of frilly which seemed foreign to me after a couple of years of fending for ourselves without a female influence. Before going to bed she wore pink slippers with little fluffy puffs on them and a flimsy nightgown and robe that you could see right through. And, she smelled like she had gone overboard on the perfume or bath powder. Dad was a cosmetics salesman and he had taught us not to overdo it with fragrances. I wondered if he thought she had put on too much, too.

She tried to be real friendly but hugged us like she knew us and called us sweeties. It felt like she didn't know how to be around kids.

We went with Dad the next day to several of his sales calls and then went back home to Fullerton. In the car Dad asked how we liked that lady whose name I can't remember. We all three said that she was kind of creepy although she had tried to be nice. Gently and briefly Dad added that one day there would probably be a woman who would become a part of his life and ours.

When Dad said he was bringing Sallie home for dinner I was both hopeful and scared. Where did he meet her? At Longs Drug in Fullerton. What does she do there? She's the cosmetics buyer and salesperson. Does she like kids? Yes, she has three girls of her own. How old are they? About the same ages as you three girls. What are their names? Shannon, Jamie and Dana. Does she know that you have a bunch of kids? Yes, she is eager to meet you all. Do we have to hug her? Just be polite.

Dad drove down to Garden Grove to pick-up Sallie that night. When he walked in the backdoor with her he wore a big smile and she, too, smiled brightly as he introduced her to each of us: Bob, Mike, Steve, Cindy, Debby, Laury. She marveled at all of our tennis trophies displayed on the mantles that ran the lengths of three walls of the dining room. Later she would say how intimidated she had felt by all those trophies. We all had seemed so competent to her and quite the closely-knit team.

She looked like a movie star. She had sparkling blue eyes, wore a tight, low-cut, spaghetti strap dress, bright red lipstick and her black hair was pulled back tightly in a carefully styled pony tail. We girls wore ponytails, but hers looked different, much more stylish.

As we all whispered in the other room my brothers Bob and Mike said that she was really young. I hadn't noticed, but she *was* young, just 29 years old, twelve years Dad's junior. Bob said that she was only twelve years older than he was.

Dad had fixed his best menu: pork roast, oven grilled potatoes, applesauce, green peas, and ambrosia salad. We did behave and presented our best version of polite. She asked some naïve questions about all of our sports, but she seemed to be genuinely interested. Dad smiled a lot so that was a good sign. He seemed happy.

After dinner we started to clean up and Sallie and Dad said that they would take care of it. That was a treat.

We girls went back to our bedroom and agreed that Sallie seemed like a nice lady. Debby said how pretty she was. We had a jewelry making kit and one of us suggested that maybe we could make her something.

She would probably like that. So we set to work. The earrings in the kit were based on little cork half spheres. Using tiny little pins we attached miniature sequins to the bases. Then earring clasps were to be glued to the backs.

We hadn't used this kit before and it was taking much longer than expected. Dad came back to our room, said that he was going to take Sallie home, and to come say goodbye. We told him in chorus that he had to wait a few minutes. We had something for her but it wasn't ready yet.

Steve looked into our room and said that he would help. Dad said OK if it just took a few minutes. With Steve lending a hand we were able to finish up, although the glue still seemed a little wet.

The four of us rushed out to the kitchen and gave Sallie the surprise. We had found a small, empty, perfume-bottle gift box and carefully arranged the earrings inside. She opened the box and was thrilled with our offering. Steve said, "Wait a minute." He ran and got our camera and asked that I take a picture of him with Sallie. I still have that picture. They are both smiling, she wearing the new earrings.

Six Plus Three

After Dad had introduced us to Sallie it was obvious that he was serious about her. He had a home office and for many years was in the habit of nightly taking the orders he had written down to the Fullerton post office. Methodically, yet sweetly, he would tuck us in and say, "I'll be back in a few minutes," and he always was. Once he started seeing Sallie, however, he would drive down to her house in Garden Grove most nights, although he would still say, "I'm going to run down to the post office." I remember lying awake until I heard his car come back up the driveway.

We all knew that soon we would be meeting Sallie's three girls. My earliest recollection of them was at their home in Garden Grove. It must have been summer. The girls were dressed in shorts and halter-tops. They were beautiful like their mom, and I felt sort of plain and young and out of my element.

Sallie was a single mother, Dad had told us that, but as a young teen I didn't really know what that meant. She had been married and divorced, but her girls didn't seem to have any father in the picture. I knew that Sallie had worked from the time she was twelve and she had always had to fend for herself. She had struggled with various health issues including tuberculosis and polio, but her spirit and outlook always seemed positive. She was very sweet to us and seemed eager to make us feel comfortable in her home.

Shannon was the oldest of Sallie's girls and confidently showed us around her house and the neighborhood. I was impressed that the other houses were so close by and that some of the neighborhood kids seemed like extended family to the girls. Shannon was about 15 and had a swagger and flare that I had never seen in any girl at my high school. Most remarkable was that Shannon was totally stunning: black hair, blue eyes and a natural, knockout figure. My sister Debby dubbed her, "of another species." Shannon was Elizabeth Taylor-style gorgeous. When Dad and Sallie were married several years later she, as the Maid of Honor, wore a sleek, olive green sheath dress. Her hair was done up in a beehive. She had a provocative style.

When we first met, for some reason, Shannon sort of took to my youngest sister Laury and me. Shannon was dubbed Number One; I was Number Two; and Laury was Number Three. I can't remember what we did together, but it was fun and different. We laughed a lot and it felt special that an older kid, who looked so grown-up took time to be with us. Boys were always calling her on the phone or driving by the house to see her. She said that she got tired of all of that.

Jamie was the middle girl, a couple of years younger than Shannon, similarly attractive, but taller. She, like Sallie, had penetrating blue eyes, dark hair and resembled Jane Russell, a movie star of the day. Jamie and Debby were the same age. I don't remember Dana too well from those early days. She was pretty young, ten or eleven. She seemed carefree and cheerful but very mature for her age. All of the girls spent long hours home without adult supervision, as did we.

We didn't see Sallie's girls very often. Now and again they would come up to the Grandview house but it was naturally a bit awkward. We had been in that house all of our lives and new players were now altering every formula we had established. I didn't envy Sallie's girls the role of trying to fit into such an entrenched household culture. Also, it was all too obvious that Mike and Steve were taken with Shannon's good looks and allure.

One day Dad asked me to go with him to look at some new houses that were being built in Fullerton off of State College Blvd. The homes were beautiful, with large kitchens and family rooms and oversized bathrooms. The bedrooms, however, were tiny as were the backyards. It felt as if one house was built on top of the next and that neighbors could look right into each other's houses. I asked him why we would want to buy a new house. Without saying that he was planning to remarry, he said that it might be hard to fit "all of the kids" into our house.

So after years of living apart but wanting to be together, Dad and Sallie married in August of 1963. All nine of us children, ages 10-20 were in the wedding. I was 16. Five of us six girls wore matching blue dresses and Shannon wore the green sheath. It was a simple church ceremony in the not so simple Garden Grove Community Church, which later grew into the Crystal Cathedral. Dad and Sallie wanted to have the Hawaiian Wedding Song played during the service but the pastor said No, it was a secular song.

The newlyweds honeymooned in Hawaii and I have no memory of all of us in the house on Grandview Avenue that week they were gone. I do remember heading back to school. Shannon "commuted" to Garden Grove High School for her senior year and the boys headed off to college, Bob to UC Berkeley, Mike to UC Santa Barbara, and Steve, who had just converted to Mormonism to BYU. Jamie joined my sister Debby and me at Sunny Hills High in Fullerton. My sister Laury and Dana went to Wilshire Junior High.

With six girls in the house, from two different upbringings, and of wide-ranging, disparate personalities, it was only natural that there were plenty of opportunities for disharmony, and disharmonies there were. Sallie tried her best to be mother to all of us, but Dad always stopped shy of embracing Sallie's girls as his own. Both Dad and Sallie were long accustomed to being the only parent and naturally protective of their own. Whenever we would go to him with problems related to the blending of the two families he would tell us "just let it go" or "don't make waves." We never gelled into a "Brady Bunch;" problems that arose were rarely resolved.

Perhaps a new beginning, with a new house for us all would have provided a more even playing field, but the decision was to bring all of the family together in the Grandview house. Sallie dove into remodeling the house. The master bedroom was the first project, which made good sense to me. Room by room Grandview started to grow away from the original '50's décor. The breakfast bar where we all had sat in a row was gone as was the circular bar and the cupboards that had held all of our books and toys and games. The trophy shelves came down, as did the mantle. New kitchen cabinets were painted brown and orange. The chop block in the center of the kitchen remained, but it, too, was painted.

Long overdue repairs followed: carpets were replaced, walls painted and broken windows fixed. A new dining room table replaced the octagonal poker table and Sallie prepared regular sit-down meals. The simple menus we kids had fixed with weekly repetition gave way to hot breakfasts, prepared sandwiches at lunch, and elaborate multi-dish suppers. There was bread and butter on the table with every meal and fresh vegetables, green salads, iced tea, milk and tons of leftovers.

Somehow bedrooms were allocated. Debby and Laury shared a room, Sallie's girls were in what had been the boys' room, and the garage became a makeshift bunkroom for the boys when they were home from college. What had been the study became my room. I was free to decorate it the way I chose, and it had a door to the patio. On Saturday mornings I would sleep-in and Dad would methodically sweep the red cement of the patio. "I'm not bothering you am I?" he would tease. "I wouldn't want to wake you up."

There were only a couple of years that all of "Sallie's girls" and "Bob's girls" shared the same house. The boys, for the most part, were away at college or in an apartment on Malvern Avenue. At one point, for reasons unbeknownst to me, Sallie and her girls abruptly moved out into an apartment of their own. There was a kitchen fire in the apartment and they moved back to the Grandview house. I moved out of the house when I was 19. One by one all of the other girls moved out, too.

Dad and Sallie, although they maintained an abiding love, eventually divorced. Soon before Dad died in 2006 I asked him if he and Sallie had ever talked about how they were going to meld those two families: six kids plus three kids was an enormous challenge to take on. "No," he said. "We might have tried to talk about it a little bit, but we figured that things would just work themselves out."

IT'S ALL RELATIVE

Sports and competitiveness were abiding themes in our family. When we were kids Dad made sure that we all learned a good game of tennis, and he taught some of us golf, too. The boys played Little League and later joined various sports teams in high school. As a little girl I was envious of my brothers' uniforms and cleats and fans in the bleachers. This was the pre-Title IX era, and the only girls' team in town was fast pitch softball. Somehow I had been silently taught that girls from our neighborhood didn't travel to the other side of town to play in that league.

But the opportunity to play on a team and wear a uniform, of sorts, and wear cleats came around in the '80's. I was a young mother of two and my husband Jim and I had moved back to California from Pittsburgh, Pennsylvania. It was great to be around the Hall family again, and when asked to join a coed softball team with some of my brothers and sisters the answer was a quick and certain "Yes."

Our team was "The Rowdies" and we wore black and white t-shirts with the team name printed on the front. Many of us had young kids at the time and they wore their little "Rowdies" shirts as they played in the dirt around the sides of the diamonds. My nephew Adam was the team doctor. He was only five years old or so, but he loved to dress up in costumes and he would come to the games complete with white jacket, stethoscope and blood pressure cuff. The games could get pretty rough, so we didn't let any of the kids be ball boy.

We played in a City of Fullerton recreational league, but being Hall Kids we took it pretty seriously. Our team wasn't all family, but it included all five of my brothers and sisters and two brothers-in-law, too. We had team parties at the end of each season, and we named an MVP, and

Most Improved Player each season. With only a certain number of teams allowable, my sister Debby would sometimes line up at City Hall for hours to ensure that the "Rowdies" would be included. My brother Bob's wife Becky was our General Manager and she kept team stats long before there were computers to spit out batting averages and slugging percentages. Becky has since died of cancer, and it is an enduring image of her sitting in the stands filling in the play-by-play book. She had her own way of scoring. There were nights that I went four-for-four without getting a ball out of the infield. In Becky's book a walk was a hit; and if you reached first on an error that was a hit, too.

Dad was in his seventies. He was the owner, since he paid for the registration fees and some of the t-shirts, too. On occasion he or Becky was called on to play catcher or take a turn at bat for the team. Forfeiting was not an option. Losing wasn't an option, either. The "Rowdies" became a dynasty: we were champs for thirteen seasons in a row—two seasons a year. Our focus was so intense that during one game when my daughter Melina cut her tongue while playing on the teeter-totter, we waited until the end of the game to take her to the Emergency Room. (There *was* a nurse in the stands who checked out the injury and assured us that waiting an hour or so would not do any harm.)

One season's championship was threatened by a late season challenge from our rivals, "Sorroc." For some reason I was called upon to pitch, and I had worked all week to learn the slow pitch style that simply demanded that I get the ball a certain height before dropping in or around the plate. Practice was a little shaky, but I knew I had to come through.

The trouble started in the first inning when I walked two batters. "Sorroc" was determined to exploit that weakness and decided, as a team, not to swing unless there were two strikes on the batter. My aim went from bad to worse and before too long I had walked in several runs and I was so tight in my delivery that pitches were going behind the batters. It wasn't pretty. Walks led to runs and more runs. I had walked in more than a dozen runs when I turned to my brother Bob who was playing shortstop and said, "You better pitch. This isn't working." He told me that I could do it. It was OK. His faith in me was honorable but misplaced.

We scored runs to equal their tally, but my walks were killing us. Finally, my brother realized that if I stayed on as pitcher we would lose the game on walked-in runs alone. Bob finally took over as pitcher and his strikes made "Sorroc" batters swing, and we made the outs. The score was still tight. In the deciding inning my little sister Debby raced toward home for a critical run. She ran into and through the young lady playing catcher who was a checker at the Lucky Market where Debby shopped. It was a critical run but not enough to secure the win. These many years later Debby is still a bit embarrassed about that aggressive play.

Towards the very end of the game brother Bob got into an altercation over a close call at the plate, argued heatedly with the umpire and threw his bat into the fencing. We not only lost the game, but Bob was suspended for two games. We won the championship, as I recall, but the season showed us that our competitiveness had gone too far. Was ploughing people down and throwing bats really what we wanted to model for our own children? The "Rowdies" soon disbanded, although other men's teams and co-ed teams followed.

In the 1990's sister Debby came up with the idea to start a new family team that could include our next generation, several of whom were over 18 and thus eligible to play. A bit of brainstorming led to the team name: "It's All Relative." This team would not be as cutthroat as "The Rowdies", although excellence in effort and performance was assumed. Going out in the field wearing the "It's All Relative" aqua and white t-shirts felt good. Playing second base I saw my sister as catcher, brother as pitcher, brother-in-law as first baseman, nephew as shortstop, sister as third-baseperson, nephew in left field, brother in center field, partner in right field and brother as rover. Our opponents, once they discovered that we were all family, made the false assumption that we would be easy prey. They were quickly surprised. We could make the hits and we could make the plays, and we had each others' backs.

My throws from second to first, for instance, went into a slump. I was reassigned to play rover, and when men were at bat the rover served as a fourth outfielder. Fielding grounders and line drives and getting the ball to the infield went well, but catching fly balls under the lights was more challenging than I thought it would be. On more than a few occasions, I thought I had the ball in my sights, ready for a relatively easy out. At the last instant I would realize that the ball was going to sail over my head. But with my speedy nephew Joey to my right, I knew that I could holler, "Joey, it's yours!" And there he would be sweeping in to make the catch.

Joey is one of thirteen nephews and nieces. Some are closer to each other than others, but they all know, as have we six siblings all these years, that there will always be family there for them—no questions asked.

CORNELL AVENUE

As a kid, Cornell Avenue was where I went to the dentist. As a young mother it was where I raised two children, and as a grownup daughter it's where I visited my aging dad. As Dad reached his 80's, dementia and limited sight made it unsafe for him to stay at his home on Grandview Avenue, even with family help and a personal care assistant. For 24/7 care we six brothers and sisters sought the best environment for him: a home-style facility that would provide him with safety, nurturing, comfort and stimulation. We finally located a small, well-kept home on Cornell Avenue in Fullerton, just two miles from the Grandview home. The owners hired a Filipino couple to live in the house to provide three meals a day, some dressing and bathing assistance and a clean, cheerful atmosphere for up to four residents.

We took Dad to visit the Cornell house, and before weighing in on the final decision, I drove with him up to the Grandview house. We walked around and he sat on his well-worn lawn chair in the driveway. "What do you think, Dad? Would you rather stay here or go to the home on Cornell?" He smiled but didn't answer. He looked at me as if to say, "You decide. I'm not even sure of the question."

At Cornell Dad had his own room with his own furniture, clothes, some personal items and a few photos on the walls. When I would visit him he was usually in the front room with the other residents. He would get up to eat or go to the bathroom or to have a cigarette in the garage. The TV was usually on. There was a schedule of recreational activities posted prominently on the wall along with the number to call if ombudsman assistance were ever needed. I never saw any activities being conducted, but JR and Lulu, the caregivers, were kind and attentive.

The roster of residents changed all too frequently. I lived six hours away, in Northern California, and it seemed that each time I would visit there would be an empty chair or one filled by a new resident. "What happened to Harold or Maude or Hazel or Ruby?" became a question for JR or Lulu, because Dad never had an answer. Dad was one of the healthier residents. He ate well, could walk around the house with the aid of a walker, and rarely complained of aches or pains. He had no disease and took few prescriptions. He didn't interact much, however. With limited vision, hearing, and mobility his world had become quite small. After lunch he would relish walking to the open garage and sitting with JR to have a cigarette. He was allowed four a day and he would often ask if it was time for a smoke.

Sometimes when I would visit I would converse more with the other residents than with Dad. I felt guilty, but I found myself wishing that he would talk more, like Doris, for instance. Cheerful and chatty, she was one of the ladies who shared Cornell with Dad for more than a year. She told us that she loved to sing and that in her younger days she was quite the dancer. She told us about her family and how she used to work as an executive secretary for a very successful businessman. She had been a fast typist and could take dictation, too. Her face was always animated and she seemed to follow the news on TV and always had the daily paper on her lap. Visible in the pouch of her walker were crossword puzzles from the paper, folded tidily.

I told Doris that I loved crossword puzzles, too. "Oh, yes," she smiled. "I do one every day. It keeps me sharp." Dad used to read the paper everyday and had been a devotee of the Sunday news shows. He once said that he had dreamed of being the Governor of North Dakota. He didn't read the paper anymore, and only the grandest of stories on TV would gain his attention. Maybe if Dad were able to read, or follow the news, or do crossword puzzles he would be more engaged and engaging?

One day when I visited Dad, Doris was not there. Her daughter had taken her to the doctor, although her walker was still by her chair in the living room. I wondered which crossword puzzle was her favorite. Mine was the "Los Angeles Times" Sunday Calendar puzzler with lots of puns. I hesitated but then took out one of her puzzles. She hadn't started it yet.

Then I looked at the other ones folded in the pouch and saw that there was not one letter in one square in one puzzle.

Doris passed away while Dad still lived at Cornell. I would have wanted to go to her funeral, but folks at Cornell would be well gone before any of us would be notified. I still do my "LA Times" puzzle every week, but I do muse if one day I will fold them up, unsolved, and put them in the pocket of my wheelchair for others to find.

THE COWBOY PLATES

When Dad's health started to deteriorate, we six kids had regular meetings to discuss issues regarding his well-being. Some years before macular degeneration started taking Dad's eyesight and before dementia started taking his lucidity, Dad and his second wife Sallie had divorced, so the decision-making regarding Dad's care came to us. Since our mother had died when we were very young, we were used to banding together in times of need.

We had years to warm up to the most difficult Dad decisions such as whether or not to authorize a Do Not Resuscitate Order; whether or not to continue his dialysis; and, in the end, whether or not to hospitalize an ailing Dad when he came down with pneumonia. The "warm-up" decisions included when to take away the car keys, when it was no longer safe for him to live in his house alone, and when to move him to an assisted care environment. We always sought his input, but he would say, "Whatever you kids think is best."

In making these decisions we six always worked together until we came to a unanimous "vote." Each of us had veto authority. Moving Dad out of the Grandview house, for instance, was a tough decision, but safety concerns finally prevailed.

We divided up the tasks of getting an appraisal, choosing a broker and putting the house on the market. Laury, the youngest, and the President of the "Hall Family Council" since she was seven years old, carried much of the detail work, as did Aunt Becky, oldest brother Bob's wife, who worked in a bank. The house, which had seen us through so many eras, was up for sale. We moved a few pieces of Dad's furniture into his room at the Cornell Avenue assisted living home. Over the years he had cleaned out the house pretty thoroughly, but what to do with what remained?

We knew what we didn't want to do. For ten years or more we had heard phone calls between Dad and his two brothers, Jim and Bill. Repeatedly they would argue about Grandma Hall's modest savings and possessions. There was one item that was the focus of the many conversations: her diamond cocktail ring that resided in a safety deposit box, which was controlled by Dad. Every six months or so Uncle Bill would call and say that he should have the ring, or that Dad should sell the ring and distribute the funds among the three boys. Dad would argue that Grandma had lent money to Bill, which he never repaid. Uncle Jim would agree. No money for Bill. Over and over this conversation persisted.

When it came time to distribute Dad's possessions, we six kids and our spouses got together up at Dad's house, 1010 Grandview. Our first agreement was that whatever process we chose, we would not let it devolve into any animosity. No possessions were worth sibling being angry with sibling.

Someone suggested a lottery of sorts, and the idea took off. For each item in the house, each of us would decide if we were interested in it or not. If interested, we would put our name in a hat. For one article there might be six names, for another four, and so on. For each item one name would be drawn among the interested parties. In this way we would walk through the house with the hat and the slips of papers with our names on them, and let the combination of choice and chance decide what would go to whom.

Aunt Becky volunteered that perhaps a more nuanced, failsafe process was needed. Perhaps, if one sibling's name was chosen more than three times in a row, then that name should not be placed in the hat for the next drawing. Somehow we six knew that to tinker with the simple system originally proposed would be detrimental. The more clear-cut the better. We also agreed, gently, that no in-law voices or opinions would be allowed. Each sibling needed to decide individually if he or she was interested in a certain item. So, we all agreed. Just the voices of we six, no in-law input, and no intricate rules.

There were, however, two exceptions agreed to regarding the lottery. Each of us would take our own Christmas cup with our name on it, even though it was part of a Santa Punch Bowl set, and each of us would have one of the ceramic plates made by artist friend of the family, Myrton Purkiss. We began the evening by drawing our names out of the hat to see in which order we would choose our favorite ceramic plate. In each of our homes we have our "Myrton" plate predominantly displayed.

So the lottery began. Steve's name seemed to come up the most: the bumper pool table; the antique, white-metal sliding outdoor furniture; the cowboy beds; the Santa Punch Bowl; the wicker furniture. We started to laugh, because everything he "bid" on seemed to come to him.

Laury ended up with the heavy chop block that had been the center of kitchen conversations and activity for fifty years; the cement patio pieces with our handprints and signatures from the early 1950's; and Dad's wooden desk.

My name prevailed for the metal waste basket that sat under Dad's desk; the wood and orange vinyl chair that Dad sat in every day for the last ten years, having his evening chamomile tea and his last cigarette of the day; an early California water color that hung in the playroom; two sets of encyclopedias, the Book of Knowledge and the Encyclopedia Americana; lots of children's books and some green cordial glasses.

When other items from the kitchen came to the lottery, the only things I hoped for, in addition to the green glasses, were the Cowboy Plates. They were heavy, restaurant ware that we had used everyday throughout our childhood. They were Wallace China, made in California in a Westward Ho, Rodeo Pattern. On each plate was a bucking bronco and its cowboy rider. The signature of artist Till Goodan was below each bronco, and a lariat surrounded the rider and horse, with western brands around that. The brands represented the working California ranches of the day, included wonderful mysteries of childhood decoding such as Lazy R; Rocking S; and Bar W.

I wonder still why I so deeply wanted one of those plates. Beyond nostalgia, perhaps it was because they were so breakable and at the same time so sturdy. A few of them had survived without a chip or a scratch. How unlikely was that in an unruly family of six barely supervised children?

Each of the six of us chose to place our name in the hat for those few remaining Cowboy Plates. One by one they were chosen; I don't remember whose names were selected, but mine wasn't.

As the evening wore on, it seemed as if the house would never empty.

One by one the siblings went off to their own homes and to their families waiting there. Shelly and I were visiting from our home in Santa Cruz, and soon we were the only ones remaining in the quiet, creaking house. "Have whatever is left, if you want anything else," the siblings had agreed. The rest would go to the Goodwill.

We did a final clean out of the garage and found some old dolls and doll clothes and even some army gear from World War II. Inside we found some old Playboy videos tucked away behind the TV; some nude photos of Marilyn Monroe in a desk drawer; some ledgers and check book stubs; and file folders from early years with DuBarry Cosmetics.

We drove home a few days later and in the quiet of the car Shelly said that it was too bad that I didn't get one of those Cowboy Plates. I agreed, but told her that it was OK.

Fewer than ten days later a UPS truck pulled up in our driveway, so reminiscent of our childhood when that big brown truck was our mother's consumer lifeline. I opened the package, marked fragile, and found a Cowboy Plate. Shelly had wasted no time finding one for me for sale on e-Bay. By now we have five of those plates, one-by-one tracked down on-line.

In our will, Shelly and I designate certain items to go to certain of our children, and a few items to be sold with the proceeds to be distributed evenly among the four of them. Not binding, of course, but we have also written a description of how the four of them could come together to have a lottery to divide up amicably any of our remaining household goods. We wonder which of them will put their names in the hat to have a chance at those Cowboy Plates.

Ball, Flag, Tree

Dad had his share of physical frailties as he hit his eighties, but it was his mental decline that was the most prominent feature of his late aging. When the signs of dementia started to set in, he agreed to visit a doctor. Dad was still living at home then, at 1010 Grandview, and my partner Shelly and I were visiting for the weekend. Dad described one of the tests that he had been given.

The doctor had told Dad that he would give him three words to remember and that at the end of the exam, he would ask Dad to repeat the words. Dad told us that the words had been extremely easy to remember, since they all related to golf: ball, flag, tree.

Some five or six months later I had a call from Dad. It was quite late. He rarely called, in part because he found it increasingly difficult to use the phone, and because I called him every Sunday evening. Those weekly calls seemed to be getting shorter and shorter; sometimes he thought he was talking to Sallie, his former, second wife. During that late night call Dad said he was having trouble going to sleep, because he couldn't get something off of his mind. He asked if I remembered his telling me about those three words. He said, "I can remember 'ball' and 'flag' but what was the third one?" Admittedly, it was only with my partner Shelly's help that I recalled that it was "tree." He sounded so relieved and thanked me over and over for the help.

Following that call, two memories flashed by, memories of Dad's mother.

I was a young teenager, and Dad had asked if I would take a drive with him. He was going to go visit his mother. I hadn't seen Grandma Hall in a year, although she lived in nearby La Habra with Uncle Bill and Aunt

Bess. As we drove I recalled the last time I had seen her. At that time I had been surprised at how much she had changed. She was bright and smiling, but she seemed as if she were somewhere else.

I had always known Grandma Hall to be an impressive piano player, and she could read sheet music beautifully. She had brought her piano with her when she had moved in with Bill and Bess several years earlier. I asked her if she would play something for me. She just smiled and didn't say anything. I helped her to the piano bench. She looked at the keys and smiled. I asked, "Do you remember how to play?" I lifted her hands from her lap to the keys. She just smiled, opened her eyes more widely, gave a little shake of her head and shrugged her shoulders.

A year later in the car with Dad I realized that we weren't going to Bess and Bill's house. We pulled up to a nursing home. Dad said, "You don't have to come in. It's not very pleasant." But I asked to go in with him. Grandma was in a hospital bed. She didn't seem to recognize either of us, didn't say a word, but she smiled. Dad shared a few words with her, gave her a kiss, as did I, and then we left.

When we returned to the car Dad didn't say anything. I asked how long Grandma had been there. "Quite awhile," he answered.

I talk with my kids about my getting older, and they realize that both Grandma Hall and Dad, their Papa, lost considerable brain power before their bodies faded. We all hope that my mind and body will thrive for many, many years to come, but we realize that my aging might include uninvited companions.

Melina and Anthony concur that Anthony will be the "team captain" of my care, if ever it is so needed, and if Shelly is not able to provide for that. Melina is "assigned" to her dad, Jim. Two years ago I asked Anthony if he would do an "inventory" of my skills every Thanksgiving to sort of test my mental agility. It would be his task, for instance, to tell me if I shouldn't be driving anymore, if I was repeating myself incessantly, if my memory was failing, or if I was perseverating about bodily functions. Anthony, who is an educator, said, "Sure, Mom! I'd be good at that!"

So far so good on the annual tests. I must admit that I get nervous about our little quizzes, and I know that Anthony changes it every year, so I can't study for it. Last year I was able to list all of the cousins in order of birth date; count backwards by seven and name the presidents from Kennedy to Obama. My reflexes are good and, although I'm paralyzed from the chest down and in a wheelchair, I'm still quite strong. At age 64 my vision and hearing are OK, too.

I have to laugh, however, when I think about my days in a rehab hospital six years ago, when the neurologists were trying to figure out what had happened to my spinal cord . . . why I was paralyzed. Two residents came into the room. One of them said, "I'm going to tell you three words and at the end of the exam I want you to tell me what they are. Ball, . . ." "Flag, tree," I jumped in.

They were very serious young doctors and neither one of them cracked a grin. The lead doctor asked how I knew what he was going to tell me. I told him about Dad and his test. The doctor then gave me three new words. At the end of the exam I was able to tell the doctor what two of his three *new* words were, but I had to guess at the third. Shelly was standing right there, and I knew that she had remembered that third word.

If later in life I am asked again to remember ball, flag, and tree, I don't think that I'll let on that I already know the words.

RICHMAN GARDENS

During Dad's final years I was living in Northern California, while my five brothers and sisters and their families all lived near Dad in Southern California. In fact, Bob, Steve, Debby and Laury were right in Fullerton where Dad lived until his death in 2006, at age 89.

Dad had lived at the Grandview house until safety issues required 24/7 assistance and monitoring. He moved into a small guest home on Cornell Avenue in Fullerton for several years, and then medical needs, including kidney disease and dementia, dictated his move to "Richman Gardens," an assisted living home for those with Alzheimer's and other memory impairments. It was a clean and bright place with good hearted, caring staff. There was a rose garden, private rooms, sitting areas, a dining hall and sunny patios. Ironically, Richman Gardens was right up the street from the Wilshire Market, where we had shopped for decades, and just around the corner from the small home that Dad and Moo had bought when they moved to Fullerton some sixty years earlier.

The family kept a schedule to ensure that Dad never went a day without someone visiting him. Three generations of family frequently stopped by, and Dad saw some of his "kids" almost every day. Regular family meetings reviewed all aspects of Dad's daily care, medical needs, and finances. Often the meetings were scheduled when I was in town and other times I would join by phone. The meetings also gave us all the opportunity to stay close to each other and to deal with challenging issues of aging, quality of life, and the emotions of watching one's parent slip away.

Since I lived further away, and my visits were only once every four to six weeks, I was often called upon to answer the question, "Did you notice any change in Dad?"

One gauge of change was the degree to which he recognized me or not. Going to see Dad, I would usually find him napping in his "Geri-chair." Sometimes he would awaken as if he sensed I was there. Other times I would say, "Hi, Dad," to prod him awake. Sometimes he would say, "Oh, hi, Cindy." Other visits he would look at me and not offer my name. On those occasions I would say "Hi, Dad," and volunteer, "It's Cindy, one of your daughters." He would then say hi and ask how I was, how the kids were, and how Jim was, although Jim and I had been divorced for over fifteen years.

Each visit he would review, through questioning, what I was up to. "Oh, you moved way up there. Why did you move so far away?" "For my work," I would explain. "Oh." And he would shake his head. I always brought a pound of See's candy for him, and part of the ritual was that he would have me tuck it away in his room.

Since my siblings wanted to know if Dad recognized me, I would sometimes ask him if he knew who I was. Some days the answer was "Cindy." Sometimes he would say, "Laury." Sometimes he would say, "Help me out here a little bit." One day he hesitated and said, "My sister?" "No, Dad," I gently corrected. "I'm Cindy, your oldest daughter. You don't have a sister." "Oooh," he said as he tightened his face in a somehow comical expression, "That wasn't a very good guess."

"Well, actually, Dad, it was a pretty good guess," I added. "You often call me 'sister,' instead of Cindy." "Oh, that's not so bad then," he smiled.

On some visits, when he seemed lucid, I would ask him what he thought about during the many hours of his day. I learned that he spent a lot of time remembering the names of the six of us. "Now Bobby is the oldest, right?" he would ask. "Yes, that's right." "And Laury is the youngest." "Yes." Then there was Mike. And Steve. And you. And then Debby." "Yes, that's right." "That's a lot of kids," he would say with a deep breath.

Remarkably, he always seemed to be clear that my daughter was Melina; that Debby's daughter-in-law was Melanie; and that Bob's daughter-in-law was Michelle. He always had a good eye, and so it turned out, a good memory for beautiful, young women.

Between monthly visits there were phone calls every Sunday. I would call or Debby or Laury would call me when they were visiting and hand Dad the phone. I can picture his struggling to feel comfortable with the miniature-ness of the cell phones.

"Hello, Dad. It's Cindy."
"Who?"
"It's Cindy."
"Oh, Hi. Thanks for calling."
"How are you, Dad?"
"Good. How are you?"
"Good."
"Well, thanks for calling."
"You're welcome, Dad. I love you very much."
"I love you, too. Thanks for calling."

I loved to hear his voice. It never sounded feeble, but warm and loving.

Dad's several years at Richman Gardens included trips every other day by Medi-van to go to a dialysis facility. There were many wrenching family discussions regarding these multi-hour treatments. Were they too extreme a medical intervention? If Dad were clear-minded would he choose to have them? One Friday night, after an extended round of conversations we six were all in agreement that we would no longer send Dad for dialysis.

The next morning Laury called me from Richman Gardens to tell me that Dad had died. It was as if we had all been spared worrying if stopping dialysis was the right thing to do or not. He was gone. I pictured him lying in his room, his final breath leaving him more still than life allows.

I pictured how he would sit in the room just outside his bedroom in the building he shared with two other residents. Both of those men stayed in their rooms all day long. Their wives would come to visit them, although they no longer knew who those women were. One of the men would moan loudly and often.

One day when I was visiting Dad he had said, seemingly with great sympathy and some pain, “I don’t think those boys are doing too well. I don’t think they are going to make it.”

I think that Dad knew that he had done very well and that he would make it.

The Hall Kids, Easter, 1954
R to L: Bobby, Mikey, Stevey, Cindy, Debby, Laury

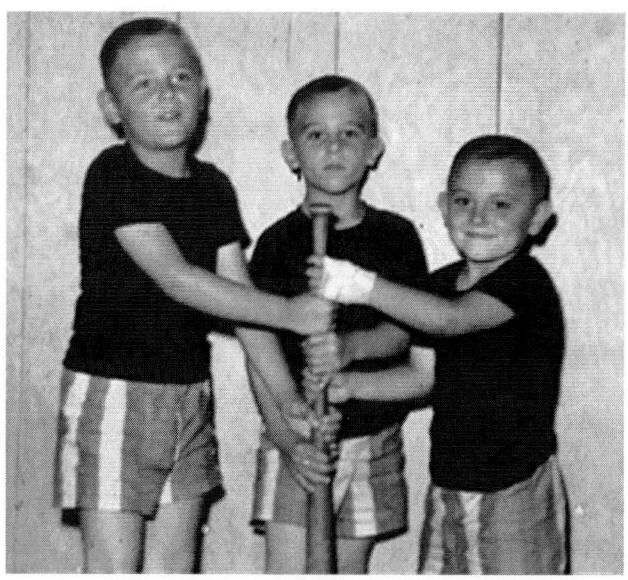

The Hall boys, 1951, in their matching sports outfits and classic buzz haircuts.

From l to r: Debby, Stevey, Cindy, Dad, Moo, Laury, Bobby and Mikey, in the Grandview dining room

The Hall Family, 1951, in the playroom of their new Grandview home. (l-r) Bobby, Mikey, Moo, Debby, Stevey, Cindy, Laury and Dad

Helen McGarvey and Bob Hall on their wedding day in Los Angeles, January 10, 1941

Bob Hall, 1945

Sallie and Dad in San Diego, circa 1964

Six Hall Kids in Their Sixties: (l to r) Steve, Laury, Debby, Mike, Cindy and Bob

Helen McGarvey, 1941

One of the ceramic plates by family friend, landscape architect and artist Myrton Purkiss.

Part Two

Here and There

UUSIKAUPUNKI

I hadn't really planned on traveling overseas when I put my name in the running to be a foreign exchange student. A few of my friends were applying with the American Field Service Program, and an adult volunteer had also suggested that I would be a strong candidate. I was 16, a junior in high school, and I didn't even like to spend the night away from home. But I wrote an essay on why I should be selected to spend the summer abroad, got Dad and Sallie's OK, and soon I was a finalist. Following a panel interview in which I convinced everyone how much I wanted to experience a foreign culture, I was chosen to go to Finland for the summer. Grateful that I had not been selected for the school year program, I also realized that I had gone too far to back out. Years later I would apply for and interview for jobs that I wasn't sure I wanted only to be faced with an offer that once accepted would change my life. So it was with the Finland opportunity. I kept my fears to myself, feigned enthusiasm, and focused on following the checklists for preparing for my trip.

My stepmother Sallie seemed very excited for me. Throughout that summer in Finland and later on during my many other travels she was the most avid reader of my letters and the most attentive listener to my stories upon my returns home. She traveled vicariously through me she would often say. As I geared up for that first trip in 1964, Sallie's exuberance began to rub off on me and I realized that I had fallen into a great opportunity. Besides, it wasn't really the whole summer—just six weeks. I bought a journal, a small atlas, gifts for my host Finnish family, and I began to research where I was going.

The adventure started with my first trip on an airplane and a night spent in a small hotel room in New York City. I don't remember how I got from the airport to Manhattan, but my fearless naïveté included negotiating the chaos of an enormous bus terminal. Once checked into the hotel room I chose to walk for hours to soak up the city atmosphere, and the next morning I somehow arrived at the dock where the "Seven Seas" awaited. Six hundred teenagers boarded the ship and set sail for the ten-day voyage to Rotterdam. During the not so luxurious passage we studied the geography, history, culture and language of the country we would visit, and I managed to come down with tonsillitis that kept me in sickbay for several days. Significantly, Jim Ranii, who would later be my husband, was also a student on that ship. He was going to Austria. We never met then or on the return voyage, but our shared experiences formed the core of our first conversation five years later.

I expected to meet my Finnish "family" at the airport in Helsinki, but only the 18 year-old daughter, Kirsti, came to retrieve me. Frowning, she let me know, in halting English, that having an exchange student for the summer was her mother's idea, not hers. She had plans for the summer with her friends and she hoped that I wouldn't get in the way. I felt disheartened, and I worried about what I had gotten myself into. We spent the night in the family apartment in Helsinki and then took a two-hour train ride and then a bus to Uusikaupunki, the location of the family's modest summer home. The rest of the family—father, mother, sister and two brothers were already there. I began to realize that in Finland even middle class families had summer homes and almost every worker had six weeks off a year to "re-create." It was my first hint that perhaps the United States was not Number One in all categories.

At the summer home I was introduced to relying on candlelight and lanterns after the sun finally set in this land of the midnight sun, using an outhouse, bicycling a mile to the bakery to buy bread each day, pitching hay, making our own yogurt, picking blueberries and then helping to make blueberry tarts, muffins, pies and jam, taking a weekly sauna with all the females in the family, and picnicking daily on the shore of a picturesque lake. One day it was hot by Finnish standards and Kirsti's mother took off her blouse and served us lunch in her bra. This was a different culture, I realized. Kirsti's English improved quickly and her disdain for me dissipated just as rapidly. Soon we were good friends and we plotted a trip to Sweden so that she would be free of her family for a week. Besides Finnish and English Kirsti also spoke Swedish, German and French, a feat that she thought of as commonplace. Maybe our educational system wasn't Number One, either. The little bit of Finnish that I was learning gave me remarkable access to enriching encounters, enormous goodwill, and an appetite for languages and cultures that served me well for a lifetime. On our trip Kirsti's ability to switch cultures and languages was on full display. In one coffee house she used all five of her languages while chatting with world travelers. Also, she was beautiful and had already, at age 18, worked as a model in TV commercials for shower soap. Boys, and men, flocked to her for attention. We spent one night on a yacht with two young men from San Francisco who were sailing around the world. I wasn't quite ready for all that happened that night, but my life view had expanded forever.

In traveling, Kirsti was fearless. I would think of her years later and was emboldened when I left India for Bangkok, Saigon, Hong Kong and Okinawa with only an airline ticket, a shoulder bag and $20 in my pocket.

At the end of the six weeks I was wishing I could stay longer, and Kirsti and I promised each other that the next summer she would come and stay with our family in Fullerton, California. She did come to stay with us and she and my brother Mike fell in love. Ultimately they didn't marry, but Mike did visit her in Finland. Several years ago, more than 30 years after that exchange program, she came to visit California with one of her grown sons and her husband. They, too, were gorgeous. We joked about our escapades that summer when we were teenagers and I recounted how eye opening the Uusikaupunki experience had been. She laughed to think that such a tiny farming village could have possibly influenced anyone in a positive manner.

She now lives in the Helsinki apartment that had been her parents. Her children are grown, successful, multi-lingual of course, and sophisticated world travelers. I picture that apartment, the same fourth floor walk-up where I spent my first night abroad wondering what I had done.

1967

It was my classmate Bettie Landauer who arranged the train trip that would take us from Delhi to Jaipur to Bombay to Hyderabad to Calcutta and Benares and back to Delhi. We six Junior Year Abroad students were on winter holiday from Delhi University. We traveled third class and were young enough not to mind the crowds, the discomforts, and the delays uncommon to an American. I was more of a spontaneous traveler, but I couldn't pass up this three-week trip that Bettie had engineered.

Bettie's father, who owned a surgical supply company that did business in India, was somehow able to pull strings from seven thousand, five hundred miles away in Madison, Wisconsin. Train tickets and accommodations were hard to come by in 1967 India, but Bettie and her dad made it happen.

Several months earlier when I had told my dad that I had been accepted to this "Year in India Program" he asked only "Is it safe?" I know only from later conversations that he worried about many of his kids that year, but he didn't burden us with any voiced reservations or fears. I am older *now* than he was *then*, so I can imagine that he and his second wife Sallie had many late night talks filled with concern about our well-being and, at times, I'm sure, our sanity.

My life's journey with India had begun in 1960 when I first babysat for the family across the street from our 1010 Grandview home in Fullerton, California. The parents jokingly referred to themselves as "American Indians." They attended the Vedanta Society of Southern California where Swamis from India gave Sunday sermons and presented classes on the Bhagavad-Gita, the Upanishads, the teachings of Sri Ramakrishna and the connections among the world's great religions and philosophies.

Author Christopher Isherwood was a regular there, as was Gerald Heard and Aldous Huxley.

It was usually on a weeknight that I would babysit their four children. When the mom and dad, Al and Meg, returned we would sit in the quiet of the living room in their modern, glass-walled home and talk Indian philosophy. I read hungrily and found an intellectual home with Vedantic thought. Soon I was going with them to the Vedanta temple in Los Angeles. After one year at Cal State Fullerton, I headed off to UC Berkeley in 1966 for my sophomore year. I was excited to see that they offered Hindi-Urdu, and I signed up for the 8 a.m., five mornings a week language classes, and a year later I was in India.

After three months of university seminars, we headed out on our train adventure. In those days in India, third class train compartments were designed for nine passengers. They were outfitted with three layers of bunks, the top two tiers of which were designed to fold up during the day. Passengers would arrive with heavy, bulky sleeping rolls, food packages, bundles of goods, suitcases, and hot plates. When counting passengers children were never included, and the idea of nine passengers per compartment was simply that—an idea.

On one stretch of our trip I counted 21 passengers in our compartment. Sitting awake one night with the black soot from the locomotive coming in through the metal bars of the windows, I tried mentally to untangle all of the legs and arms and torsos, but I could not with any certainty determine what belonged to whom. Passengers became close to one another. They shared shoulders, laps, food, water, tea, and stories.

It was during long stretches of these train rides that my classmates and I learned more about each other and our families, and having the largest family among the group, I found myself relaying stories about all of my brothers and sisters. As I told these stories in English to my classmates they would laugh or respond in other animated ways and the Indian passengers would ask what I had said. Using my elementary Hindi I would do my best to render the vignette into Hindi. A few snapshots from my shoulder bag, and the concrete language and universal emotions of family life allowed my meager Hindi to stretch to limits never reached in class.

The stories were from half a globe away, but the passengers joined me in my journey through childhood's laughter and sorrow and fear and loss, through a family coming together in times of hardship and kids drifting to far corners of the globe as young adults. They asked questions of great insight and offered their sympathy and hopes for a good life for me and for my family. As some passengers left the train and others entered the compartment, the remaining passengers would bring them up-to-date on the stories' narratives. The language they used to recap the stories was much more sophisticated than that which I had used, and sometimes I could barely follow the re-telling.

When I told them about what my brothers and sisters were doing as I was studying and traveling in India, they found some things hard to believe. It was incredible enough that a 20 year-old, still single woman was traveling so far from home. When they learned that my oldest brother Bob was in the US Army in Okinawa they asked why. I tried my best to explain the draft with its Vietnam War era lottery. I said that he had a low number so he had to go to the Army although he didn't want to go. I tried to explain how he opposed the war, that he had considered moving to Canada and how he tried to fail his induction physical by staying up nights on end and taking dangerous combinations of drugs.

But why was he in Okinawa if the war is in Vietnam? I explained in my elementary Hindi:

Bob sits at a desk. He reads reports about US Army trucks in the war in Vietnam. He decides if they are very badly damaged, badly damaged, or just a little damaged. If they are very badly damaged, Bob sends a report to Vietnam to say, "Don't use the truck. Throw it away." If it is badly damaged he sends a report to say, "Send the truck to Saigon to fix." If it is just a little damaged he sends a report to say, "Fix the truck, and use it again."

Then they would exclaim that he must be a very skilled mechanic, and I would have to explain that "No, he doesn't know anything about cars or trucks."

They would ask why did they send the reports to Okinawa? Why didn't American soldiers in Vietnam decide what to do with the damaged trucks? I had no answer, because there was no rational answer.

Next I would tell them about my brother Mike. He was in Law School at Harvard University. Many of them had heard of Harvard. "That's a very good school." The passengers always agreed that he would earn excellent money. Lawyers didn't have to work with their hands and they could find good wives. "There are too many lawyers in India," they would add. "They make lawsuits last years and years just to have work." I would show them Mike's picture and unanimously they would agree that he was very handsome and would marry well.

"But why isn't he in this lottery?" Well, I would explain, he is a student so he doesn't have to go in the Army now. After school he would serve in the Army Reserves. He would be trained as a soldier but he probably wouldn't have to go fight. "But if there is a war why doesn't he have to go to the war? If they already have too many people in the Army, then why do they have more people enter the Army? Why have soldiers in reserve? Why have a lawyer in the Army?" And then they would ask the question for which I had no answer: "Why is the US Army in Vietnam?"

Then I would tell about my brother Steve. He, too, is in the Army. "Oh, so he had a low number." No, but he volunteered to be in the Army for three years. He and two of his friends figured that he would have to go into the Army during the war, so that it would be better to enlist. They could serve together and have non-combat, specialized, safe jobs. As it turned out they didn't serve together. I told them that Steve is stationed in Vietnam. He sorts mail. When he went on vacation in Australia (called "R and R" or Rest and Recreation) several of his barracks-mates were killed by Viet Cong rocket attacks. "How could he go on vacation if he is in the Army?" That's the way the Army does it. "The hand of God kept him safe," they would say with true relief.

As for my sisters, I shared, they were both in my hometown living with my dad and stepmother. Debby is going to Fullerton College, because Dad didn't have enough money to send her away to her college of choice. "Why isn't she married?" She hasn't found anyone whom she wants to marry. "But she's out of secondary school; your father needs to find her someone to marry. He should find someone for you to marry, too."

And the youngest sister, Laury, I would tell them, is finishing high school and living at home. "That's good. She should be home helping your stepmother. She shouldn't marry until Debby and you marry."

And the stories would go on interspersed with the telling of fortunes using palm reading. They would read my fortune and then I would look at their palms and tell their fortunes, too. Of course, I didn't know the first thing about reading palms, but the passengers seemed genuinely impressed with my predictions. I would purchase sweets and fruit through the windows at the stops and share them among the passengers. They shared rice and chapattis and curried vegetables with us. The children sat on our laps and played with our hair. Then some of the passengers would look again at my family pictures and ask to have a certain tale repeated. Usually there would be one passenger who was more skilled than the others at understanding my Hindi. She, or sometimes he, would "translate" for the others. The stories took on great embellishments and cultural transformations.

After the train trip we students returned to the university and the other passengers returned to their cities, towns, and villages. I bet they would be happy to know that I was able to visit Bob in Okinawa. I saw him with his stoned eyes hidden behind blue tinted sunglasses sorting through all of those reports about trucks in Vietnam and realizing there was no making sense of his work. They would have been happy to know that I even visited Steve in Vietnam. They would have marveled at the 60 pounds of body weight he put on trying to camouflage his intense fear and anxiety.

They would have been intrigued to know that I had fallen in love with an Indian named Ashok, and they would have delighted in stories of his dashing style, his shameful brushes with the law, and his escapades with this young, foreign woman. They would have bobbed their heads and clicked their tongues and sympathized with me to hear of the protracted "movie reels" of grief that I felt having to leave him as I returned to the States.

They would have wished all of us girls well in finding husbands, which we did, although without Dad's help. They would have been happy to learn that Bob and Steve survived the Army years without physical harm, and they would have understood that other scars are still with them. And they would have said, "Oh, yes!" to hear that Mike made good money as a lawyer and married very well.

MUNGLI AND GOOMTY

I met Mungli and Goomty the second day that I moved into my room near the University of Delhi. Most of the girls in our program were assigned rooms at the university dorm, or hostel, as it was called, but they were short two rooms and I was quick to volunteer to live off campus. I thought that living in a room in an Indian family's home would provide a richer cultural experience and also be better for improving my Hindi. It was August, 1967. I was twenty years old.

It turned out that the room was in a building owned by the Varma's. Their living quarters were downstairs; I lived in a small room on the second floor, and Carol, another American student, lived on the third floor. Mrs. Varma introduced me to the "washerwoman" and the "sweeper". They would take care of my clothes and my room. They would come everyday. Their services were part of the rent but I should give them a tip every week or so. Also, any extra food or clothing that I might want to give them was OK, but not to be given too often.

That first day I said hello to these two tiny, weathered ladies whose ages were impossible to discern. They spoke Hindi in a manner I had not studied in class, but we laughed and smiled and I gathered that they would be back the next morning. I jotted down words they had used that I didn't understand and started my own little glossary of everyday Hindi. I had a special notebook for that purpose, and I was excited to get started. Digging into my dictionaries I was energized and focused.

I had always loved school and stationery and books and puzzles. When I was barely six I had started a "school" in the playhouse that my parents had built for me. I think that my mother had envisioned a playhouse for tea parties and dolls, but I had set-up a chalkboard and little chairs and workbooks and pencils and erasers and insisted that my two little sisters and other pre-schoolers in the neighborhood attend my school. I was a very serious teacher and felt that their readiness for kindergarten was in my hands.

In my small room in Delhi I set up my study space, happy to be my own teacher as I dug into my lexicons and guides to idioms, preparing for my upcoming conversations with the washerwoman and the sweeper. That next morning, however, the women didn't come. Instead, two little girls arrived. They were probably eight and ten years old. Later, I asked them their ages, but they didn't know when they had been born.

Mungli, the younger one, was one of the sweeper's daughters. Goomty was one of the washerwoman's daughters. They told me that their mothers wouldn't come that day and that they would do the sweeping and washing. I asked if their moms were Ok. Oh, yes, fine. Just not coming today.

I explained that I had just moved in and that I didn't have any wash to be done and the room didn't need cleaning. Mungli said that the floor needed swept and washed everyday. She squatted on the floor with a whisk-type broom and started sweeping. Goomty was talking the whole time, but I found it hard to follow her. They both were laughing; so were their eyes. Mungli had a simply beautiful face, always bright. Even this many years later I can easily recall her energy and constant smile. Goomty looked a bit more mischievous and would sometimes anger unexpectedly.

The second day the girls came to my room I was sitting at my desk. Mungli came in and started to sweep. With my feet still under the desk, she scooted under the desk and was sweeping under me. I didn't know what to do. My discomfort was almost painful. It's clean, it's clean, I told her.

I asked about their mothers. They wouldn't be coming today.

The girls and I came to know each other. They asked what village I had come from, and with a map of the world I tried to explain where the USA was. Goomty would argue with Mungli about whether or not California was near Calcutta or further away. There was a mirror in my room and they would look at themselves everyday and laugh and laugh, making faces and looking back over their shoulders to see if they were still there in the glass. Now and again they would see a folk performance of an Indian classical story, and they would re-enact scenes complete with character voices.

I had a sleeping bag rolled up in the corner of the room, and one day they joked taking turns walking around the room and up and down the stairs with it on their heads. They made up elaborate fantasies about being a maharani with a headdress full of jewels. I happened to say that it was impressive how they could hold the sleeping bag so steady on their heads. It's nothing, they said, anybody could do that. I told them that I couldn't. They didn't believe me until I tried. Walking across the room I was OK, but up and down the stairs I had no chance. They thought I was joking. Then they had me try it with an apple, a banana, a book. They screeched with laughter!

Among my books were some Hindi primers which I had bought at the bazaar. I had found that using them to work on my Hindi was a really pleasurable way to advance my skills step by step. They also had the advantage of being great cultural primers. Mungli, particularly, was interested in those little paperback books. She knew that they contained writing, but she couldn't read any of it. Neither could Goomty. Little by little I started to teach Mungli the Devanagri alphabet. She learned quickly. Goomty said that she wasn't interested, although she always looked over Mungli's shoulder.

Once in a while their mothers would come to the room to work and tell me to be sure that the girls were doing a thorough job. Mrs. Varma would do the same. I asked each of the women if the girls would be going to school in the fall. No, they don't do school.

It was obvious that neither girl had ever gone to school, although I knew that children of untouchables were no longer banned. In the new India, all students were welcome. I talked to Mungli's mother about school for Mungli, and she laughed. That would be impossible, she said. She has no books and no uniform.

I spoke with Mrs. Varma and she said that yes, Mungli could go to school if she wanted to. The new India provided education for all children. I inquired and found the local school and visited the headmistress. Yes, Mungli could attend school, of course. She would need books, a slate, pencils, a notebook, a uniform and shoes.

Those things were easy and fun to acquire and only cost the equivalent of a few dollars. We had the school schedule and Mungli's mother said that Mungli was very eager to start. She was appreciative of my help, but she said that she didn't think that Mungli could learn. It was agreed that Mungli would still need to do her sweeping work after school. Her mother couldn't do all of her houses without her help. There were many children in the family including a newborn baby.

For several weeks Mungli would come to my room after school. Animated, she would go over the lessons in her books. She was indeed learning to read and count and add and subtract. Goomty grew more moody and would say some harsh things to Mungli which I couldn't follow.

Then Mungli seemed to grow a bit sullen and much more quiet than usual. She would come and do her work but said that she didn't want to read to me. I asked how school was going. She said it was fine.

Skipping my university classes one morning I walked over to the school. I said hello to the headmistress and asked how Mungli was doing. Just fine, she said. There have been no complaints from the teacher. I asked if I could talk to the teacher.

Of course. She is in Room 4.

I walked across the dusty courtyard and found Room 4. As I looked in the room I saw Mungli. She wasn't sitting on the benches with the other students. She wasn't reciting the lesson with them. She was standing next to the teacher at the front of the room pouring her a glass of water. When the glass was full she walked over to the side of the room and stood silently by herself waiting for the next order.

I didn't go into the room. I didn't talk to the teacher or the headmistress. I walked home.

That afternoon when Mungli and Goomty came to work I suggested that we have our own school. We had books and paper and pencils and notebooks right here in my room. We could do a few minutes of lessons everyday after the floors were clean and the clothes washed.

That would be fine, memsahib, they said. That would be fine.

The Monsoons

It was hot. As a Southern Californian I was accustomed to that draining, wear-you-out-hot of late August that seemed to peak every year with the opening of school, but nothing had prepared me for the heat of a summer in Delhi.

As a college student on a "Junior Year in India Program," my studies at Delhi University started late in the fall, stopped often for holidays, strikes, and visits from dignitaries, and ended early in April. It was 1968, and I wasn't ready to return to the States. Piece by piece I sold my few possessions to allow me to stay longer. My small reel-to-reel tape recorder bought me two weeks; my 35-millimeter camera sponsored me for a month; my sleeping bag gave me another week; and my portable typewriter took me into late June.

Having moved out of my rented room near the university, I missed my daily routines. I especially missed having *chai* at the corner tea shack, chatting with the bicycle repairman who had a fix-it stand under a tree and teaching reading and writing to Mungli and Goomty, the young girls who cleaned my room and washed my clothes. Now I was moving from one place to another, what world travelers today would call "couch surfing." I spent some nights with a well-to-do Indian family at their house in a sprawling development of concrete and glass in New Delhi. I knew them through an exchange program that sent Indian students to the United States. The father was a mid-level civil servant and his salary provided the family with a comfortable standard of living including a fulltime cook and a fulltime driver. They also had a window air conditioner in the front room. As the heat of the summer intensified, everyone in the household would drag a sleeping roll into the front room to take an afternoon nap. When the heat became close to unbearable everyone would do the same at night: mother, father, sister, brother, and me in that small living room. One night the brother tried to be more than friendly so I found another place to sleep.

For the next several weeks I stayed with the family of a friend of a "friend." The "friend" was my boyfriend Ashok, and he was dangerously charming. Whenever he asked a favor of someone the answer was *yes*, so I had a place to stay. It was in Old Delhi, a crowded house of meandering rooms on the ground floor of a three-story building with a central courtyard. The building was made in the traditional mud brick and plaster manner and located in the midst of a maze of narrow alleyways off of one of Delhi's busiest bazaars. The tightly knit construction provided lots of shade, which protected us somewhat from the sun of the midday, but with each passing afternoon and evening hour the temperature rose. By bedtime, it was so hot that I would soak my sheets in water before getting into bed. Within an hour the sheets would be dry and I would be dripping wet with sweat. It was hot, at least 110 degrees everyday for weeks.

One popular way to combat the heat, for those of us with a few *rupees* in our pockets and time on our hands, was to go the air-conditioned movies. Bollywood was not yet thriving in the '60's but there were plenty of dubbed foreign movies and some religious and secular Hindi films. I wasn't alone in sitting to watch a movie twice, just to get out of the heat.

People didn't complain about the heat; it came every summer, and every summer the worst of the high temperatures would be broken with the arrival of the monsoons, the torrential rains that would come from the southwest. Anyone expecting a fall season in India would be greatly disappointed, because there are not four seasons but three: winter, summer and the monsoons.

The modest Old Delhi home where I was a guest had no air conditioning, and the one small fan could only run when the electricity was on—about two hours a day. Another complication was that there was a water shortage and no water was being sent through the pipes to the houses. Each household had to carry buckets down to the street corner faucet to gather its daily supply. That community faucet had water from three to five every afternoon. Surviving each day's heat became more difficult for me as the summer wore on. As my money began to run out I couldn't hide out in the air-conditioned cinemas or restaurants. I started to pay more attention to the weather forecast: "Monsoon to arrive on June 12." "Monsoon arrival late." "Monsoon due to arrive June 29."

It *would* arrive, everyone assured me. The days lengthened as people's tempers shortened. It was also the month of Ramadan, and many of the Muslims in Delhi displayed particularly short fuses as fasting and baking in the heat and fasting again collided. "The rains are just now coming," my Indian friends would tell me. "Just now coming" was a common phrase. It was also used to describe the arrival time of a train that was perhaps eight hours late.

On June 30th the skies broke, as if they simply fell apart. Crowds ran into the streets to greet the rains with dancing and chanting and outstretched arms. It was an instant festival. The steam from the hot pavement gave way to rushing water. Taxis and handcarts and rickshaws slogged through the streets and the rain soon overwhelmed the curbs. The city was awake long into the night as was I.

Finally I lay down to sleep. The temperature was actually comfortable, and I relaxed with a smile, so relieved to have made it through India's summer. Just as I closed my eyes I startled awake. Mungli and Goomty? It was still raining. It had been raining for eight hours; the streets must be flooding. What was happening to them in their handmade mud hut? The bicycle repairman? Where was he sleeping with the sidewalks underwater? The tea stall family? What about them in their shop of Coca Cola crates and movie posters?

So absorbed in my own discomfort awaiting the monsoon I hadn't given them a thought. The next day I took a scooter cab up to the University area. I went to the home where I had rented a room and found Mungli and Goomty, smiling and giggling, doing their daily work. I asked them what had happened the night before. Was everyone OK? What about their house?

"Oh, our house fell down," they said.

I was desperate for them. "What are you going to do?"

"We'll rebuild it," they said and looked at me as if I didn't know anything.

Ashby Avenue

In the fall of 1968 I returned to Berkeley for my senior year in college. Thanks to a few aerogrammes I had arranged to live with three other girls in an off campus, two-bedroom apartment. I shared my room with Laurel Edelstein. We had been dorm mates our sophomore year, and we had grown to be good friends. Our only argument had been about her refusal to dance with a German student when we went folk dancing at the International House.

Right from the start of this apartment living arrangement I realized that my discontent was not going to go away. Having spent an intense year in India, having visited brother Bob in Okinawa and brother Steve in Vietnam, returning to find Berkeley in a violent uproar over the Vietnam War and the Arab-Israeli conflict, and Governor Reagan's leaning on the university leaders to crack down on the "spoiled" students and left-wing "Communist sympathizer" faculty, I found it crazy-making to negotiate with roommates on how to split the grocery bills when some people didn't eat any of the pork chops and other people used too much toilet paper.

At the semester I got my own place, an old studio apartment on Ashby Avenue offering me the solitude I needed to try to integrate the me I had been with the me I hoped to find. I made *chapattis* (tortilla-like Indian bread) by hand, cooked up a saucepan of *dahl* (lentils) for the week, and made the place my own. I only had a suitcase full of clothes, so the tiny apartment's large walk-in closet seemed bizarre.

There was a growing sense of confrontation on the campus and in the streets. There were anti-war demonstrations that drew tens of thousands of us to cross the bay to march in San Francisco. The rhetoric of student activists was increasingly hateful and the crowds of well-educated students that cheered on the speakers' poorly thought-out diatribes were disconcerting. Police were called "pigs" and spat at.

I went to class and worked at the South Asia Regional Studies Research Center in the afternoons. I typed articles that graduate students had written. I also helped to compose introductions to those articles and handed them to the research professors who compiled the articles into books that *they* then published. Just out the window from my second floor workspace in an old Berkeley brownstone was a plot of land that the university had purchased, bulldozed and cleared. Earlier grand plans for university buildings had fallen through, and they were going to make it a parking lot. There were increasingly angry student and community voices opposed to that plan.

Coming home from work one day I had a letter from my brother Bob, who was stationed with the Army in Okinawa. He had a desk job as a Supply Clerk. He said that he had sent me a package, an old record player. He explained that it might need some fixing that would require my taking it apart. "Feel free to see how it works once you fix it." I thought I knew what he meant, but I wasn't certain.

When I had visited Bob in Okinawa some six months earlier, he had shared with me that he would take R and R (Rest and Recreation) trips to Thailand. Among other activities, he would buy a duffle bag full of Thai marijuana and bring it back to sell to fellow soldiers and American kids who attended the international school. He could buy dope for $15 a kilo in Bangkok, $10 a kilo from up-river farms, and sell it for $100 a kilo in Okinawa. It was easy money. The Army paid for his flights via Military Air Command hops as long as Bob was in uniform. "Very scary," he would tell me later, traveling with 10-15 kilos of "ganja" while on active duty.

During my visit to Okinawa, Bob had said that he might send me some "stash" to hang on to for him. Several weeks after Bob's letter had arrived, I received a notice that there was a package that needed to be picked up at the post office. Now it was my turn to be "very scared."

As I went to the post office I was as paranoid as if I had smoked some ganja. I rode down there on my 50 cc scooter and couldn't help looking in the rearview mirror to see if I was being followed. The same feeling inside the post office. I figured that if the FBI was going to arrest me they would wait until I had taken possession of the package. That's when it would happen. Maybe on the curb as I strapped the package to the back of my scooter. But nothing happened at the post office. I drove home and set the brown-paper-wrapped package on the kitchen table, my only table. I started to open it and then feared that someone might be spying on me from the window. I went into the closet and opened the package there. Yes, it was a record player. Compact, and ready to play 45's. It looked run of the mill. It didn't smell like dope. There were four screws holding down the turntable itself. I went to the kitchen and rummaged for a screwdriver, checked the windows, and went back into the closet. Opening the top of the turntable there it was: seven or eight clear bags full of pot, some of it loose and some of it in the form of "Thai sticks." I exhaled, closed the box and tucked it among my meager wardrobe.

I wrote a letter to Bob letting him know that I had received his package, that I planned to try out the "the record player," and that I would keep it for him for when he returned home. It was indeed a powerful package that he had sent. It was the people Bob sent my way, however, that is the reason I can never forget Ashby Avenue.

Bob had mentioned that he might send some army buddies to stay with me as they first arrived stateside and before they headed home. Berkeley was just up the freeway from the Oakland Induction Center, which was also the site of soldiers mustering out from the service. Hundreds of soldiers came in and out of there everyday, and it was the site of many angry protests and arrests. I was little prepared for those visits of Bob's army friends. One young man seemed to be on speed. He would talk to me long into the night, go to anti-war demonstrations during the day and come back to the apartment for more talking. He, and all the others, said that Bob was like a guru and the smartest person they had ever met.

It was Bob's friend Mike Dunham who was most unforgettable and haunting, even some forty years later. Mike mustered out and came to stay with me for a few days. As had the others, he said how much he honored Bob, how much he hated the war, how violated he had felt to be drafted, how screwed the government was, and how relieved he was to be out of the f . . . ing army. He would get stoned and talk long into the night. One night he started chanting, "Ice cream, f . . . ing chocolate ice cream." Then he would laugh. Then he would cry. He told me that the only reason he had made it out of Vietnam was because of f . . . ing chocolate ice cream.

He was in the infantry, drafted out of Salem, Oregon and sent to Vietnam for a one-year tour of duty. He and his platoon would sweep jungle areas looking to "clear out the enemy." They rarely could see the Viet Cong or the NLF (National Front for the Liberation of South Vietnam), but mines, booby traps and snipers were common. Terror gripped everyone.

"Ice cream, f . . . ing chocolate ice cream." One day food had been helicoptered into the bush for Mike and his company. He ate his lunch and went to the chow line to get some dessert. A sniper shot him. Mike was hit in the upper thigh, airlifted for emergency medical treatment and then sent to Okinawa where he met my brother Bob. In my apartment, early in 1969 Mike kept repeating how f . . . ing absurd it was to have f . . . ing ice cream in a f . . . ing war, in a f . . . ing jungle, let alone to be f . . . ing shot, in the f . . . ing butt waiting to be served some f . . . ing ice cream!

In Berkeley Mike would wander the campus during the day and had a hard time sleeping at night. He would retell the story about being shot, and I felt that there was much more to tell. He was an articulate and thoughtful guy. He raged against our government for sending him and his buddies to Vietnam, to that insanity. At times he would put his head on my lap and just cry.

One day I came back from class and my job typing research articles and saw that Mike's things were gone. I was a bit worried but assumed that he was on his way to Oregon. He wasn't the first of the vets who came through my apartment who would just sort of disappear. I went into the bathroom and saw, scrawled in lipstick on the mirror: "Screw the government."

Not long after Mike left, Berkeley, itself, became the place of bullets and teargas and unchecked violence. Outside my office window I saw the confrontations in what would become People's Park. Three times we had to evacuate our building because National Guardsmen and Alameda Sheriff's Officers had used teargas to disperse crowds that threatened to "take back" the vacant, now fenced-in lot. During one of those evacuations I saw a young woman pushing a stroller, and both she and her toddler were crying and rubbing their eyes from the teargas. I decided to leave Berkeley.

Recently I was thinking about those visitors to Ashby Avenue, and I talked to my brother about Mike Dunham. I learned that he had been the hippy of his platoon, but that he also chose to "walk point," actually preferring that in-front role to following behind. On one of those forays into the bush he had come face to face with a young Viet Cong soldier. Each raised his rifle at the other. One was going to die. Mike shot first. He recovered photos of a wife and young kid from the dead soldier's clothes. That incident haunted Mike the rest of his life.

In 1969 on Ashby Avenue I didn't know that Mike's company was Charlie Company, the same Company in which Lieutenant William Calley served. Mike's injury was one of 28 incidents, including five deaths, suffered by that company in a short period of time. Mike's shot in the buttocks while waiting to be served chocolate ice cream was part of what precipitated his company's actions to retaliate against the VC. Those actions included what we later knew as the My Lai massacre. Some 400 unarmed Vietnamese were killed, including women, children, babies and the elderly. Calley, a platoon leader, was later convicted of murder. Mike had been airlifted for medical treatment before his company was sent to clear out the village of My Lai.

These many years later I wonder if Mike had remembered those few days on Ashby Avenue. I wonder if he remembered the cry of rage smeared on the mirror. I wonder what had happened to him. To what degree had he recovered from the war? Had he ever recovered?

My brother tells me that Mike died of liver failure six months ago, at age 66. He had stayed in Salem, Oregon, living in a small house his grandmother had given him. Mike had "holed up" in that small house all these years, living off of government checks and volunteering as a vets' counselor at the V.A. Hospital. He had two children, but never married. Neighbors knew his place as the one with the copies of scratched-out government regulations plastered on the front of the house and anti-government signs posted in the yard. I can only assume that smeared on one of those signs was the message: "Screw the government."

Peesh-kesh

My husband Jim and I joined the Peace Corps after graduate school, and we served in Iran for three years, two years as volunteers and one year as staffers to train new volunteers. We lived in the city of Kerman, a provincial capital in the center of the country. At the time, 1971-1974, Kerman was a city of 100,000 residents, most of whom were Muslims but with a smattering of Jews, Zoroastrians, and Christians. There were 200 Russians who had come to Kerman to build a cement factory, but they lived in a fenced compound outside the city.

Jim and I were the only Americans in town, and there were two Brits, the Episcopalian pastor and his wife. Jim worked in the City Planning/ Engineering Office and I taught school, grades kindergarten through high school. The Minister of Education had decided that as many students as possible should have an English-speaking English teacher. The other English teachers didn't speak English, although English was a required part of the curriculum.

We were quite the oddity in town. We lived in a lovely but modest home in the Zoroastrian area, a five-cent taxi ride from the town square and its ancient bazaar. The landlord, Mr. Azjadhi, served as our gardener and he arranged for a housekeeper and a woman to wash our dishes every night and our clothes every week. We liked to say that we lived in "Spartan luxury." We had to heat water every Friday for a weekly shower, but our assignment was far from the well-digging, village-based assignments that were the stereotype of the early Peace Corps years.

We learned Farsi, shopped in the local bazaar, visited with our neighbors, played backgammon for long hours into the night with friends, ate pistachios, melons and seeds, and drank strong tea which we sipped from our tea saucers through cubes of sugar placed in our mouths. We went to Farsi films and American films in Farsi, tuned into the BBC at night when we could find clear reception on our shortwave radio, wrote letters home and read dozens of books. Life was leisurely and work hours relatively short although we worked six days a week with Fridays off.

One of our dearest friends was Abu. He worked in the same office as Jim. He was a draftsman of considerable talent and was preparing for a series of exams that could qualify him for promotion. He had developed elaborate methods to cheat on the exams which seemed to require much more effort than studying for the exams would have entailed. Abu came by almost every day. He was patient with our nascent Farsi, and he also was our guide to all things Persian. He tutored us in the elaborate system of Iranian "*ta-arof*". *Ta-arof* is a complex of polite words, phrases, and exchanges that are culturally required of any social exchange.

If one enters a room, for instance, there are phrases that must be said to insist that the other person with you enter first. When you meet a friend there are phrases that must be shared to inquire as to their well being, that of their spouse, their children, and their parents. When a bill comes at a restaurant there are phrases that are exchanged with vigor to decide who will pay the bill. A bill would **never** be split. I loved *ta-arof* phrases such as "Your servant," "May your shadow never shorten," "May your hand not pain you." One of my favorites was "*peesh-kesh*."

Peesh-kesh roughly means "it is yours" or "take it". Its most common use is when someone compliments something that is yours. If I say to someone "That is a beautiful rug," he must say "*Peesh-kesh*." The rules of *ta-arof* dictate that the owner of the item must insist, with feigned sincerity, that he really wants you to have the complimented item. Stories are told of foreigners succumbing to such offers and leaving Iranian homes with jewelry, clothing, or even a carpet.

Our friend Abu regularly offered us all that he had. "That's a nice watch you are wearing." *Peesh-kesh*, he would say as he took the watch off of his wrist. It would take a verbal struggle to make him put the watch back on his wrist. He would try to give us his cigarettes, his books, his jacket, his fresh bread from the corner shop, his drafting pencils, anything for which we noted the slightest interest.

During the highest of holy days, Abu would go to the mosque, say his prayers and listen to the mullahs. As many in Kerman, Abu was not a staunch Muslim. He didn't say his prayers five times a day; he couldn't read Arabic; he couldn't recite the Koran; he liked to smoke, drink vodka, watch movies and meet foreigners. He followed all things American through imported magazines and he was hungry to know all about our lives in the States. One afternoon he came to the house straight from the mosque. He was extremely upset and struggling with what the mullah had preached. He said he knew that we were good people, but we were not Muslims. "If you are infidels, and all infidels are bad people and will be confined to Hell, how can you be good people? If you aren't Muslims you can't be good people." He was so pained trying to reconcile his personal experience with what was being preached to him. The only "out" he found was to assume that someday we would convert to Islam. In that way our friendship could continue.

All three of us were in our mid-twenties, and Abu often asked why we didn't have any children, although we had been married for more than a year. This was a common question in Iran. Why wouldn't a young couple have children? For the first month or two we had tried to explain that we didn't plan on having children right away. We were enjoying our time together without the responsibility of kids. Also, we explained, we weren't certain that we wanted to have children. The world was in turmoil. There was war in Vietnam and disruption at home. We soon realized that these responses only puzzled people and led to conversations more complex than our basic Farsi could handle. We took to saying, "We are trying. Hopefully we will have a baby soon, '*Insha'Allah*', Lord willing."

Abu was very concerned that we didn't have a baby. Every few months he would ask in a variety of round about ways, insuring the appropriate level of modesty, if I were pregnant. One day he seemed particularly distracted and I worried that he was again struggling with the Muslim/Non-Muslim dilemma. Jim was in the garden and Abu asked if he could talk with me alone in the kitchen.

He stumbled for words but said that he hoped I realized that he and I were good friends and that he counted Jim as his very best friend in the world. He wanted us to be happy and he wanted *Allah* to bless us in our lives. I thought that he was going to plead with me to convert to Islam, but then he went on to ask if I was in good health. Was Jim in good health? "There must be something wrong physically, because you have been here for more than a year and you aren't yet having a child." Taken aback, I then heard the ultimate *peesh-kesh*. "If I can be of service to you and Jim, I am happy to give you myself as a sexual partner. This could be with or without Jim knowing."

Part Three

Moving On

The Onset

(This piece was first published in the "Journal of the Transverse Myelitis Association," January 22, 2008.)

How does one start to tell a life-changing story? In the case of the story of my onset of Transverse Myelitis, I don't even now when the story begins. Was it with our fairytale trip to Scotland in July of 2005? Was it with the coughing and sneezing children in the plane to Ireland? Was it the first sign of a backache a few days after we returned? Was it the loss of feeling in my left foot and my falling over on top of a glass coffee table? More than likely the beginning of the story is something I will never know, when some unknown virus entered my body and started the mysterious chain reaction that led to my being a paraplegic (T-3, complete, ASIA—A).

Late in July of 2005 my partner Shelly and I and other members of our family had just returned from Scotland where we had participated in our daughter's destination wedding. A castle in Scotland, men in kilts, and a stunning bride made for a never to be forgotten event. Also, we had played golf five or six times including at the home of golf, St. Andrew's. Returning to California we spent a couple of days at a resort near San Diego, California. I played golf once there before our drive back up the coast to Santa Cruz.

All seemed well when we returned home, and we were happy to play with grandchildren, and I remember lifting them over my shoulders and running down the hallway of our house. When I awoke with a backache in the middle of the night I attributed it to lugging golf clubs halfway around the world, being cramped in cars and planes, and carrying grandchildren around on the unforgiving hardwood over cement floors. My 58 year-old body would bounce back, I was sure, but I knew it might take a day or two.

I got out of bed that Monday morning, did some yoga poses, which I did every morning, and willed myself to get back to work. I trusted that being active would do the trick for my post-travel back stiffness. My work as superintendent of a high school district was busy and demanding, and I was returning to it after the first full three weeks off in many years.

Throughout the day, however, the pain did not go away. That night I was unable to sleep. I tried sleeping on the floor, which gave me some relief. I went to work again on Tuesday. Again, at night the pain was intense, and I stayed home from work on Wednesday, and arranged to see my doctor on Thursday.

Leaving the house on Thursday for my doctor's appointment I reached for my briefcase by the front door and fell backwards onto the floor bumping my head on a coffee table. Never before had I ever fallen. My left foot had just buckled under me like it was asleep. I drove the 30 minutes to work and worked for an hour or so to catch up on some issues, before driving to the doctor's office. The doctor had been called away to deliver a baby, and I was told I could reschedule. I said that I would wait however long the wait might be. I somehow knew that something was going on, but I had no idea what it was.

I saw the doctor an hour or so later. She was seriously concerned but unable to diagnose what the source of the backache and loose left foot was. She prescribed pain medication (Vicodin) and an anti-inflammatory (steroid) and said, "I don't think you have had a stroke." A stroke? I had never even considered that what was going on could be really serious. I had assumed a pinched nerve or a "tweaked" back and that a trip to the chiropractor or the doctor would put me back in shape. The doctor said not to go to a chiropractor until we had determined what was going on. She also said that if the pain worsened or if I lost control of bowel or bladder to get to the emergency room right away. That sounded ominous. I still assumed, however, that the post-travel backache and foot looseness was temporary.

I went to the pharmacy to fill the prescriptions, and while waiting in line I realized that I was not able to stand without wobbling. I asked someone to hold my place in line, and I went to the cane aisle and picked out a cane. I sat on a bench near the pharmacy counter until it was my turn, and with the help of the cane (which I purchased, by the way) I made it back out to the car and home.

Immediately I took the medications and lay down on the couch hoping for some relief to the now excruciating back pain. Unfortunately, within two hours, the pain had worsened, and I was unable to control my bladder. I called our health insurance hotline and the nurse confirmed that I should get to the Emergency Room *stat.*

Shelly drove me to the Good Samaritan Hospital in Los Gatos, and using the cane, I was able to walk. My left foot was slightly drooped and dragging and my back hurt like crazy. I checked in with the triage nurse and then found a comfortable place in the waiting room, along with some 10-20 other people. I knew from experience that it would be a long wait, and I was readying myself physically and psychologically for an extended stretch of sitting. My first sense of "oh, no" was when the triage nurse called my name ahead of everyone else's.

The nurse put me in a hospital bed in the ER and doctors of various specialties came in right away and performed multiple tests. Within several hours I had seen a neurologist, orthopedic surgeon and a cardiologist. The orthopedist and the cardiologist each announced to us that I was fine, as far as their specialties went. With smiles, each of them left for the evening—not their case on a late evening in the ER.

The neurologist was puzzled, although he assumed that I had probably had a stroke. I was admitted to the hospital for further observation and testing and to make me comfortable. After an MRI and other tests the neurologist concluded that I had had a stroke in my spine, a spinal infarction. He made calls to a local rehab center and suggested that I would be best to go there for a week or two and that I should regain the movement of my left foot within 4-6 weeks. It would take some work, but I should be fine.

I met with the president of my school district's Board of Trustees and we named an acting superintendent, because it looked like I would be out of commission for several weeks. I was using a walker in the hospital. Some friends and family visited and we even had an impromptu birthday party on the patio for a dear friend. On the way back to my room, using the walker I walked with my three-year-old grandson. We arrived at my room and I started to go in. He said, "Let's go down to the end of the hall and back." I was totally out of energy but the grandma in me agreed. As we got to the door of the room he looked up and said, "We'll get you back, Grammy." That was on a Friday, and it was the last time I ever walked.

Over the weekend the lack of feeling in my left foot moved upwards and soon I could no longer move my left foot or leg. Also, my right leg lost its sensory function. I was doing range of motion exercises the best I could, and I awoke in the middle of the night on Sunday night. I thought that since I was awake anyway I might as well do the range of motion exercises. My feet and legs, however, did not answer the call. I could not feel or move either leg, and my midriff also had no feeling. I lay there alone and whispered to myself, "Oh, sh—. I'm screwed."

I saw the neurologist the next morning and he seemed truly perplexed. He said that he would transfer me to a larger regional hospital, Stanford University. He didn't know what I had or what to do about it.

At this point my body went into "spinal shock" and two weeks of intense pain ensued. It was after three weeks of hospitalization that the terms Transverse Myelitis were first used to describe my condition, although the neurologist noted that my presenting signs were neither transverse nor myelitis. Some say that there is no worse fate than being a medical anomaly in a teaching hospital. The doctors concluded that my case was probably prompted by an unknown virus, thus my case was idiopathic. Dozens of doctors were interested in my case, but the focus was on describing my case not on treating it. All treatment focused on controlling the pain and protecting my bodily systems. After the pain had been put under control, I was told that I would be transferred to Valley Medical Center to its spinal cord injury rehabilitation center. It is then that it became clear to me that there was no treatment for my condition, but that my focus would now be on learning how to live with it.

That was reconfirmed when I settled into my room at the rehab center. A nursing assistant was taking some vital signs and asked, "How long have you been a paraplegic?" I actually started to turn around to see whom she was addressing. It was a long, sobering moment when I realized that she was, of course, talking to me.

Many chapters of my life have been lived since my "onset" story of two and a half years ago. As of this writing I am 60 years old with more grandchildren and more time to enjoy them. Although I returned to work after six months I am now retired. I work out at a rehab gym twice a week, play wheelchair tennis, some golf, and enjoy the increased space in my life. Shelly and I have put 26,000 miles on a Toyota Sienna ramp van which is fitted with hand controls for me, and we have made the necessary modifications in our home to make it accessible and comfortable. We are a four wheelchair family: manual chair for most days, power chair for long outings or when my elbows and wrists act up, a commode chair for toileting and showering, and my favorite, the tennis sports chair. Our life has changed dramatically, but with Shelly's positive spirit and the love and help of wonderful family, friends, and neighbors, we have been able to move on and embrace life. It's more difficult, of course, but I have also found that I am more patient, kinder to others, and more appreciative of all that life offers.

If I can be of any help to any TMers or their loved ones, please do not hesitate to get in touch with me. I can be reached at cranii@me.com. Life does come at us sometimes.

Rehab

(*This piece was first published in "New Mobility Magazine," February, 2012 under the title "One Room: Two Worlds."*)

It was both distressing and a relief to be transferred from the acute care neurological wing at Stanford Hospital to the Spinal Cord Injury Rehabilitation Center at Valley Medical Center in San Jose. It marked the beginning of the realization that there was nothing the doctors could do for my paralysis, but it also marked the beginning of my recovery. It was the summer of 2005, and there were about a dozen of us in the rehab wing, all trying to come to grips with our abruptly altered bodies.

Most spinal cord injury patients are men, and there was only one other woman in that two-corridor first floor wing. My roommate, Maria, looked like a teenager, and she had been in a terrible car crash. Part of a large migrant worker family, she was one of eight passengers in a van, heading to the fields early one morning. The van had been blind-sided in an intersection, and Maria, who wasn't wearing a seatbelt, was the most severely injured among those passengers. One person in the other car had been killed. Maria had come through several surgeries and wore a neck and back brace and a metal "halo" while her spinal fusions took hold. She, like me, was paralyzed from the chest down and would use a wheelchair for the rest of her life. Maria and her family spoke Spanish, and daily I would hear her talking through the drawn curtains with her many visitors, including her husband and her little boy who was barely two-years old.

As a school superintendent I often reflected on and analyzed bureaucratic systems, the sophistication that is sometimes needed to navigate complex organizations, and how a lack of knowledge of English can make those navigational tasks even more challenging. Watching Maria and her family try to work within the rehab system confirmed my concerns. Valley Med had an elaborate interpreter service, and when it worked well it could be impressive. If a non-Spanish speaking nurse or doctor or social worker needed to speak with Maria, he or she would call for an interpreter. Some of these requests were pre-arranged and some were impromptu; some were in person and some were by telephone. The rehab staff seemed to have a list of objectives that each of us had to meet before we could be discharged. One of these topics was "Sexual Issues and Paralysis." This educational unit included a social worker meeting with each patient to discuss sexual functions and habits, pre- and post-injury. There was no privacy for Maria and her young husband when they met with the social worker and the interpreter to discuss topics that would be embarrassing to anybody, let alone a young, soft-spoken, traditional, Hispanic couple. Even more embarrassing for the young couple was the lesson that had to be translated for them sentence by sentence that taught the young husband how to manually assist his wife in what was euphemistically called a bowel program.

I remember the quick "yes" that Maria would answer when the social worker time and again asked if she understood a particular point. The husband's "yes" responses were even quicker. I felt badly for them in so many ways. They were so young, and their lives had been so shattered. I was 58 years old and had already enjoyed a robust physical life; I had raised two children, enjoyed the successes of a substantial career and was relishing the role of Grandma. Maria and her husband were barely in their twenties. Sometimes in the evening I would hear Maria cry softly, and my compassionate partner Shelly would go over to her, hold her and help her to wipe away her tears.

Any one of us in the rehab ward would have turned back the clock if we could have, and none of us was above hoping that there was some cure or miracle that would make the neurons in our spines start talking to our brains again. Many well-wishers said they were praying for me and that they knew that my strength as an individual would see me through this ordeal. If anyone could walk again, *I* could, or so I was often told. My condition, an acute onset of Transverse Myelitis, *did* include the possibility of some recovery, but for some reason I knew from the start that the lesions on my spine would never be repaired. Maria's condition was such that she, too, assumed that the wheelchair would be her companion for the rest of her life. These realizations, however, did not stop us from embracing any suggested intervention.

A friend of ours said that she knew of a spiritual healer who had experienced remarkable results with other patients. Realizing that there was nothing to lose, I agreed to a visit from the healer. At the same time, Maria's family was arranging for a prayer circle to convene around her bed. As the healer arrived a few minutes before seven, the first of the prayer circle family and friends started to arrive on the other side of the room. There were at least 18 visitors, by my count of feet under the pulled curtain. Children ran in and out of the room, laughing and playing tag.

My healer seemed disconcerted by the noise as the Spanish prayers, with their call and response patterns, started to fill the room. Shelly and I said that the noise didn't bother us at all, that any efforts to comfort were welcome. The healer began by running her hands over my body from head to toe. She didn't touch my body but kept her hands two or three inches above the skin. She said she was sensing where there were blockages that she could repair. As she came upon a blockage she would take in a deep breath and then burp loudly. We tried our best to be respectful of this seemingly odd technique, so we had to be careful not to catch each other's eyes too often. The impetus to laugh was strong, but willing to admit that maybe this healer had some magic to impart, we restrained ourselves.

In the meantime the prayer session on the other side of the room was gaining in volume. The choral prayers were followed by singing and a long sermon from a minister. My limited Spanish told me that the speaker was calling upon the healing powers of God to visit Maria, to make her whole, to bless her and her family. Concurrently my healer continued to breathe and burp and breathe and burp. As she completed her 45-minute session I thanked her and asked what she had "read." There had been great stress, she said, and she hoped that her intervention would create new pathways of peace. When she told me that the session cost $60 I lost any trace of faith I might have generously granted her.

The prayer session went on for another 90 minutes. Participants started to file out of the room and the curtain was drawn back. A staff person rolled in a TV with a VCR player. The leader was explaining that it would be most helpful for Maria to watch the videotape set that he was leaving for her. She should watch it at least twice a day, everyday. Before going to bed, Maria used the remote control to start the first tape. It was the "Video Bible." It was complete with actors dressed in biblical clothing and a narrator whose deep voice filled the hospital wing. The tape series started with the Old Testament and a preponderance of scenes included shepherds and their flocks. "Baa, baa, baaaaaaa," the sheep bleated. Above that, the narrator, in Spanish, went on with his telling of Bible stories. In the morning "Baa, baa, baaaaaa" greeted me. In the evening "Baa, baa, baaaaaaa" competed with the evening news or a baseball game or the hospital educational channel.

With any other hospital stay I would have insisted that my roommate turn off the VCR, or at least I would have asked the hospital staff to do so. I was tempted to do that, but Maria was just so young, and her husband was so young, and their little boy was barely two years old.

DEATH BY *EMPANADA*

Empanada*: a turnover or mold of pastry filled with chopped or ground meat, vegetables, fruit, etc., and usually baked or fried.*

When we were kids our parents would take us to the Snack Shop on Friday nights for burgers and shrimp and chopped steak. After our mother died, instead of the trip to the Snack Shop, Dad would sometimes take the six of us to La Chiquita, a Mexican restaurant on Maple Avenue near downtown Fullerton. Maple ran through the "Mexican part" of town, and going to a *barrio* restaurant felt adventuresome. We heard Spanish being spoken, and items on the menu included *menudo, mole,* and *pozole.* I ordered tacos and homemade tortillas—safe and familiar. La Chiquita was also the first place where I saw children working. The kids of the owners would clear off and re-set tables and then go back to their homework.

Not far from La Chiquita, on Harbor Ave., was another Mexican restaurant called El Comedor. On occasion Dad would take us there, and it was my first experience with a restaurant that used tablecloths, dimmed lighting, and male servers. I would not stray from my tacos and tortillas order, but I recall that Dad would order *albóndigas* soup, *enchiladas* or *chile relleno,* and for dessert, *empanadas.* The empanadas were sprinkled with powdered sugar and when I finally tasted one, I thought they were wonderful.

Empanadas, and variations of them in other cultures, became favorites of mine. When I lived in Finland one summer as a teenage foreign exchange student, I loved their ground meat pies; in Iran, fig and fruit *kolampes,* were the signature pastry treat of the town in which we lived; and much later in life when traveling in Chile, meat and fruit empanadas were first on my list when visiting a café or bakery. The best empanadas always came hot out of the oven or the deep fryer.

In 2005, when I became paralyzed, empanadas were there to teach me a lesson. My partner Shelly and I had accepted an invitation to a Christmas party. We had inquired about accessibility, and the hostesses said that the front door was hard to reach, but there were back stairs going to the kitchen that would work for me, with the help of a few willing hands. When we arrived it was raining. One of our hostesses opened the garage door and we safely traversed slick pavement to reach the stairs: at least twelve of them ran very steeply from the garage to the kitchen. Shelly and two others safely carried me and my chair to the house, but it felt treacherous to me. Also, I worried that someone might have hurt her back or knees, and I have grown to be as concerned about the health and safety of my 'helpers' as of myself.

Once in the house I relaxed with a glass of wine and some cheese and crackers. Since it takes two hands to maneuver my chair, I balanced a small plate on my lap while juggling the wine glass. The rooms were crowded with guests, and for the first time I experienced three things about going to a cocktail party in a wheelchair: it is not easy, or even possible at times, to roam from one room to the next; it is hard to extricate from one conversation to go on to another; and it is difficult to graze for finger food. Always somewhat ill at ease at such a party, in a wheelchair I felt even more unsettled. One guest actually hung her jacket on the push handles of my chair. "You don't mind, do you?" she said. I did mind, but I couldn't find the words quickly enough to object.

I found a comfortable spot where I could sit in my chair, place my glass of wine on a coffee table, and interact with a flow of people. I reminded myself just to relax and have a good time—let the party come to me if necessary. Shelly offered to bring me a variety of hors d'oeuvres. I was delighted when I saw that dessert empanadas were hot out of the oven. One of the hostesses served me two of them, along with a napkin and the caution, "Careful, they're hot."

They were wonderfully hot. I put two napkins under the empanadas and placed them on my lap. The fruit-filled pastry helped me feel at ease, as only comfort foods can do. As the party wound down, we elicited the aid of several strong and healthy friends who managed to get me back up the stairs, down the wet driveway and to the van. It had been a successful evening, and a significant first social outing since I had come home from spinal cord rehab.

Home and in bed, changing into pajamas, I noticed some redness on my thigh, just above my left knee. It puzzled me. It didn't hurt, of course, because I have no feeling, as well as no movement below my chest. The next morning I saw that the redness had given way to blisters. It looked like a burn, but from what? Then we realized that it must have been the empanadas. I called the doctor and followed her advice for burn care. In rehab, I had read and heard stories about paraplegics being unknowingly burned, and how infections could cause serious damage. I was confident that my burns were minor, but that I would have to be more cautious in the future. I could not help myself, however, from taking a moment to laugh and "write the headline:" *Paraplegic succumbs to death by empanada!*

We All Fall Down

At a wheelchair tennis tournament several years ago I saw an accomplished player head down a slope towards the scorer's table. In an instant he was on the ground, splayed out head first on the asphalt, having hit an unexpected piece of uneven pavement. Just as quickly as he had fallen he pulled his paralyzed legs towards his body, reached up to the seat of his chair and with a powerful thrust of the arms dead lifted himself back up into his chair. All of this happened before any of the dozen people heading towards him to help could reach him. I thought, "What a different experience that must be. To fall out of your chair but know that you can get yourself back up into it."

When I was in the Spinal Cord Rehabilitation Center six years ago, I watched as the Physical Therapists worked with the other patients, all but one of whom were young men. Each of them had experienced a terrible accident. The variety was sadly dramatic: a motorcycle spin-out on a wet road, being hit by a truck while changing a tire, a victim of a drive-by shooting, a head-on car crash, being thrown from a dirt bike during a race, being hit by a wave when playing in the surf, diving into a swimming pool, diving into a river while on a church-building trip to Guatemala.

My own injury was idiopathic: the doctors never figured out what caused the lesions to form on my spine. One week I was playing golf and tennis and the next week I was completely paralyzed from the chest down. The best they could do was name it: Transverse Myelitis.

In the rehab gym, where I worked out four hours a day for six weeks, I noticed that the therapists were teaching the other patients with paraplegia how to get from the floor to their chairs. After several weeks I asked why I wasn't being taught that skill; it seemed important to be able to move from any low surface, including the floor, back up into your chair. My therapist said that "Sure, we could work on that," but she seemed to put it off. I prodded her for several days and then we started to skill-build toward the goal of lifting myself back up into a chair.

But in the end, physics and physiology didn't cooperate. My arms were short in proportion to my body. My upper body weight was light compared to my lower body. Fifty-eight year old wrists and elbows and shoulders strained to the level of injury. I did learn, finally, to lift myself up to an intermediary "station", and then from there to a chair, but I have never managed to lift myself from the floor to my chair.

That all is preparatory to saying that I have been extremely cautious about falling from my chair. Once down I am dependent on others, and strong ones at that, to get me back up. I received training in rehab on how to have others assist me to return to my chair safely. That skill I have used many a time.

We were told in rehab, more by "returnees" than by the staff, that we would experience falls. Despite those testimonials, being quite a cautious and well-coordinated person, I didn't believe that I would be falling.

But fall I did. My first fall, actually it was more of a slide, came within my first few weeks at home. My daughter, Melina, had come to stay with us for a week. She was one of many who changed their schedules to help Shelly and me get through those first few months.

I was using a transfer board, and with Melina's help I was moving from the bed to my chair. Somehow my weight shifted unexpectedly and both of us could see that I was "going down." Neither of us could stop the slow motion, gentle, irreversible trip to the floor. We both started to laugh and at the same time rearrange my crumpled legs to make sure that nothing was broken.

Now what? Melina tried to lift me back up to the bed, but my 150 pounds were not to be lifted. A home-visit Physical Therapist was due in but a few minutes, so we waited. When Aneeka arrived, Melina answered the door, introduced herself and said, "Mom's fallen to the floor, maybe you can help."

Then it was the three of us having a good laugh. Aneeka sat on the bed, spread eagle and gripped me under my arms. Melina lifted my legs from below. Together they boosted me back onto the bed, my ending up on Aneeka's lap. "Hi," I said. "Very nice to meet you."

There were other falls early on. Home alone one morning I again "slipped" from the bed, this time in trying to transfer to a commode chair. The chair had moved on the hard wood floor as I was mid-transfer. I called our good friend Bob; he and his wife Fran drove over to the house immediately. After a quick lesson in the "Aneeka method," Bob sat on the bed and lifted me back up—onto his lap. A comical scene.

After several months my strength and skills improved, and transfers, which had previously taken 5-10 risky minutes became quite routine. We hired a wonderful Personal Care Assistant who helped me with shower transfers on the days Shelly was at work. I had reached a level of safety and comfort. I could even transfer in and out of cars without too much strain. Within six months "post-injury" I was on the road, with my own ramp van with hand controls. Falls, I believed, were behind me.

On a sunny, beautiful day at our home in Santa Cruz I was heading down the ramp, which we had built to the front door. Then I was on the ground, having fallen forward out of my chair. Barbara, my assistant, was only feet away, and neither of us could figure out what had happened. She called for help from Kurt, our neighbor, and together they lifted me back into my chair.

Upon inspection we saw that a welcome mat that was placed next to the beginning of the ramp, had scooted less than an inch away from the ramp itself. My front wheels had hit that mat and forward went my weight as the chair stayed where it was. No injury, just a whack to the head.

With the help of a generous friend and the Rotary Club of Los Gatos, where I was a member, we had installed a lift that took me from the house level to the street level via the garage. It was great. Independently I could get from the house to the garage to the van to the world!

One day, about a year post injury, I rolled up the short ramp onto the lift. Then I remembered that I had forgotten something in the house. My daughter-in-law Lindsay and children A.J. and Olivia were visiting, and they were in the house. I backed down the small ramp, and "boom" I fell backwards onto the cement, half in and half out of my chair. I checked for injuries, saw no bones protruding, and felt clear-headed, although the back of my head had taken a bounce as I hit the pavement.

I called for Lindsay, in a manner meant not to alarm, and reassured her that I was O.K. Grandson A.J., who was four at the time, came out of the house. He walked around me, announced, "No blood," and went back in the house. I had Lindsay retrieve Kurt from across the street and they set me upright.

Predictably there have been other falls. Twice I slipped to the van floor: once when transferring from the driver's seat to the wheelchair and once from the wheelchair to the driver's seat. The cell phone was invaluable in those instances: call Robert, call Kurt, call Rachael.

There was the fall in a driveway when we were at a real estate Open House. Six or more of us were all chatting, in a group, when I wheeled back to have better eye contact with someone who was talking. Then I was down.

One evening Shelly and I were crossing an unfamiliar street, looking for a restaurant we had not been to before. She was a stride or two ahead of me heading straight down the sidewalk. I noticed the restaurant sign and called to her and pointed to the restaurant, which was actually to the right. As I pointed and called, hands off the rims of my chair, my front casters hit a small pre-curb in the concrete and I flew head first out of my chair onto Wilshire Blvd.

Almost before I realized I was down, two strangers and Shelly were right there. I slowed down the strangers as I checked for injuries and then Shelly and I worked with them to set me back in my chair.

My most recent, but probably not my last fall, was unique, as was each of the prior ones. I had just come out from the dentist's office, and I had my transfer board on my lap. I rarely take it with me from the car, but to access the dental chair, it had been needed. Typically I would tuck the board between my right thigh and the side guard of the chair, but this time, somewhat hastily, I just put it on my lap. As usual, I lined up the chair with the ramp of the van, and pulling hard on the rims I went backwards up the ramp. I was wearing slick, polyester pants, and sitting on a shiny, new cushion on a snazzy new chair. I pushed extra hard to propel the chair. As I went up my bottom weight slid forward on the cushion and the transfer board started to slip. I must have reached for it and yes, down I went.

I was down on the protruding edge of the ramp and my lower legs were folded underneath my thighs. Shelly came around from the driver's side and we both checked for injuries. Nothing protruding. Looks OK. Shelly retrieved Sean from the dentist's office to help us, and soon we were on our way.

But I was not as lucky as I thought. Although I couldn't feel any pain, swelling and bruising told me that something was wrong. X-rays told us that I had broken my tibia and fibula. No cast was necessary, but three months in a heavy, awkward brace slowed me down considerably, particularly with transfers.

The fear factors that set in after that "last" fall have taken me almost four months to overcome, but I'm back to confidently rolling along. This week I played tennis for the first time since the broken leg and it felt invigorating and freeing.

For me, being in a chair can be a solitary and sometimes isolating condition. Overall, however, it links me more to others than my able bodied existence ever did. It is not a solo ride. We all fall down sometimes.

1-X

Clothing issues started as soon as I was transferred from the Stanford University Hospital to the spinal cord injury rehab facility in San Jose. That was six years ago, but I distinctly remember wearing a hospital gown with the Stanford logo on the front. I had always wanted to go to Stanford. But the gown quickly gave way to everyday clothes: in rehab everything was rightly geared to getting me on with my life.

For the first day or two Fillipino nursing assistants helped me get dressed. Paralyzed from the chest down I had little sense of what I could or couldn't do, and I was more than happy for their help. I recall lying in the bed looking down at my body and seeing my stomach puffed out and flabby. I had always prided myself on a firm, flat stomach, working on it with sit-ups and yoga, long distance walks, and years of diet discipline. But the abdominal muscles were now paralyzed and unable to "hold me in." I knew I couldn't walk and that my body had no feeling from the chest down, but I wasn't prepared for losing my flat tummy and trim torso.

On the third day in rehab an Occupational Therapist announced that she would come to my room each morning and teach me how to dress myself. The teaching, it turned out, included her standing by the side of my bed watching me struggle into my clothes. One day she watched me for 10 minutes tussling with my pants before I realized they were on backwards. "That's an easy mistake to make," was her only comment.

After a day or two I realized that dressing would be much easier with larger shoes, looser pants with elastic waistbands, and slip on shirts. It really bothered me that I couldn't hold in my stomach. My doctor was a wheelchair user with quadriplegia, limited use of all four limbs. (She had a surfing accident while in Med School), and I asked her about this stomach situation. "It's called Quad Tummy," she explained. She raised her loose-fitting blouse and showed me her tummy. "There's no getting rid of it. It's not fat; it's just that your body can no longer hold up all of its insides the way it once did."

I worked out at the gym each day and tried engaging the little bit of stomach muscles that still responded. And by trial and error, I learned what clothes worked and what clothes weren't worth the trouble. After six weeks in rehab I was released to go home. Shelly had installed lowered clothing racks that I could reach from my wheelchair, and soon we took off the doors of the closet, because they were so heavy for me to open. From my bed I could see my clothes: suits for work, heels, a couple of lovely evening outfits and plenty of sports clothes.

Every morning when I woke up I would look at that closet. I soon realized that most of my shoes were too tight on my seemingly perpetually swollen feet, and they would just fall off when I transferred in and out of the chair. When I was able-bodied I never realized how much we flex our toes and arches to keep our shoes in place. I started wearing tennis shoes everyday. I packed away my other shoes for the Goodwill.

Next I realized that my wheelchair would not accommodate most of my fall and winter jackets. They were too bulky behind my back and the arms were in the way as I wheeled the chair. I slowly packed them in a box, saying goodbye to each garment before sending them to family in Utah.

I planned to go back to work after about six months at home, so I was eager to start trying on some of my work clothes. I had hired a Personal Care Assistant and some mornings she would help me try on a dozen garments or more. Soon I realized that most of my blouses and jackets no longer fit. My shoulders were broader from months of working out, and my biceps and triceps were much larger. Growing strong enough to push a chair around all day had made my size 8 blouses obsolete. Also, my blouses no longer fell neatly over my stomach; they just sat there. I had my helper pack them away for the Goodwill.

Saying farewell to my collection of slacks was the hardest part of my wardrobe grieving process. Lying in bed, looking at my slacks hanging in the closet I could recall the feeling of standing. I could feel the pleasure of fabric draped down from my waist to my shoes. I could remember the feeling of shiny lining against my skin as I walked. I could hear the sound of my work shoes clicking on the floor and the pleasure of how my slacks fit against my waist. I tried on lots of my slacks. Only a few of them fit right over my new middle, and all of them were extremely difficult to pull on and off. I had my helper pack them for the Goodwill.

Slowly I discovered clothes that did work for my new body and lifestyle. They were far from fashionable, but they were functional. Until very recently my closet still held many clothes that I couldn't wear. I had often had a variety of sizes in my wardrobe, because my weight fluctuated over the years, but now I realized that those smaller sizes were never going to fit, even if I lost some weight. Grieving is a slow process.

Last week I went shopping with my daughter, Melina, who has great fashion sense and impeccable style. She was treating herself to a birthday shopping trip complete with personal shopper at Nordstrom. I joined her in the dressing room and asked the shopper to bring me some tops. I told her that I was in search of a style that actually fit my body with its substantial tummy that I couldn't hold in. "What size do you wear?" she asked. "I used to wear an 8, but now I really don't know what my size is."

The shopper brought in a variety of tops, most of which made Melina and me laugh because they were too big or too small or too fancy or just not me. But she brought in one top that was made of a lovely wool-blend fabric. It was black and gave me plenty of room for my buff arms without looking too sporty, and it gave me ample room over my tummy. "Looks pretty good," we all agreed. I looked at the label and saw that it wasn't a 10 or a 12 or even a 14; it was a 1-X.

I bought the top and on the way home stopped at Macy's. I was long overdue for some new everyday T-shirts. A saleslady asked if she could help me.

"Yes, I'm looking for some T-shirts."
"Great," she smiled. "And what size do you wear?"
I still couldn't fully accept my altered body, but I was finally able to admit, "1-X."

POSTSCRIPT

Six in Our Sixties

SIX IN OUR SIXTIES: THE HALL KIDS TODAY

Bob, the oldest of the Hall kids, is now 69, and Laury, the youngest, is 61. We all live in California and remain a tightly knit family. Thankfully, we all enjoy good health, and none of has had to struggle with the alcoholism that took our mother at such a young age. I think that we are uncommonly happy as each birthday gives us another year to embrace living.

Over the years we all married, although five of us later divorced. Two of us have painfully lost spouses to cancer. Each of us currently has a spouse or partner, so there are six wonderful significant others willing to take on the challenge of being a "Hall-in-law." Each of us has children: two each for five of us and three for Mike. I also have two sons from my partner Shelly, and two of us have grandchildren.

We all excelled in school and two of us have advanced degrees. For the most part we are retired; we have served as letter carriers, teachers, a lawyer, a school administrator, teaching assistants, bookkeepers, office managers, nannies, and personal care assistants.

Not surprisingly, sports continue to connect and sustain us in many ways, just as they did in the days of backyard football and our family softball team "It's All Relative." Bob and Debby play tennis together every week. Mike and Steve compare notes on bowling techniques, Laury plays golf with my partner Shelly, and Debby and her partner Sam coach and train me in my wheelchair tennis.

Bob is an avid slow pitch softball player and excels at the highest level of senior competition, being selected for all-tournament teams and capturing several batting championships. His batting average (as high as .805) and nearly error-free fielding are no surprise to us. He leads the family, perhaps, in single-mindedness and focus, sharply honing his skills on any chosen target until he is close to unbeatable. Once a merciless adversary, Bob has mellowed and lets the recreational aspects of sports grow. When Bob's wife Becky died two years ago he found solace in his softball teams. Accessing the Zen of sports he found "his path into the 'now'." He discovered that it was still fun to get a hit or to throw someone out at first, even if Becky was not there to watch him.

Mike, like all of the Hall boys, has excelled in multiple sports: golf, basketball, tennis, and running. In the last several years he has spent most of his sports time on golf and bowling. He has turned away from the stress of competition and turned towards finding that great feeling of the well struck three-wood or the well-rolled strike. He enjoys hitting balls at the golf range, and when he plays on the course he rarely keeps score. He has great bowling technique, guided by a weekly lesson, and in 2010 he rolled a perfect "300" game. He brings his faith in the value of sports to his three children, all of whom play tennis among other activities.

Steve, a lifelong tennis player since winning his first tournament at age eight, still plays weekly. He used to play some golf with Mike and brothers-in-law Chuck and Bill, but he has moved on to running. He has completed four marathons, each under five hours. Steve is lifetimes away from the hard-drinking, 230-pound soldier being shipped out to Vietnam. Trim and fit (he modeled for an ad in a senior fitness magazine), Steve has found that running helps to keep him physically and psychically fit. Recently he has started bowling again and competes on a men's team which, not surprisingly, won league last year.

Debby came to tennis a bit later than the older kids. She would have preferred dancing as a hobby, but born into a sports family she developed an impressive tennis game. In the 1980's Laury convinced Debby to play doubles in a tournament. The "girls," as we always called them, proved to be an effective and highly in-synch duo and enjoyed considerable success. As adult students at Fullerton College they decided to play tennis on the women's tennis team. All of their teammates and opponents were 18-19 year-old students, while Debby and Laury were in their mid '40's. Many doubles teams thought that these two ladies were coaches or perhaps mothers who had come to cheer for their daughters. The girls were underestimated when they warmed up displaying their relentless, finesse-based games. The girls' winning ways took them to the California State Championship and designations as Academic All-Americans.

Debby, at the encouragement of our dad, went on to teach tennis to many Fullerton youngsters. (Dad always had the knack of convincing us that we could do things we had never tried before.) And Debby still regularly plays tennis and paddle tennis. She stays incredibly fit and taught boot camp aerobics for four years. Debby has also competed in bowling leagues and completed four multi-day marathon walks, three to raise funds for breast cancer treatments and research.

Laury, also, is an accomplished athlete who has continued to keep sports in her life. For many years she was a standout softball player setting records with her hitting and her fielding at third base. Now Laury's sport's focus is golf. To-date, her best round is a 76, and at age 61 her handicap index went to an impressive 6.1. I have no doubt that Laury could have been a pro golfer if she had so chosen. As with Debby, the pinnacle of Laury's tennis "career" was being named an All-American as a player for Fullerton College. Debby often said that Laury's overhead was Debby's best shot. An avid walker, Laury participated in marathon walks and rarely goes a day without logging in a brisk three or four miles.

As for me, I have always loved tennis, ping-pong and walking. When I was able-bodied I played in dozens of tennis tournaments and completed five marathon walks on behalf of breast cancer charities. I loved training for those walks: working up to daylong solo outings that helped to clear my head and invigorate my body. Now that I am in a wheelchair I miss those long, quiet excursions into self, but I enjoy hatha yoga and strength training. To recapture that sense of moving my body through space and to enjoy that adrenaline kick of competition, I am active in wheelchair tennis, gaining United States Tennis Association national ranking in 2010.

Adjusting to some of the realities of aging, I am beginning to focus more of my sports time on table tennis, playing three days a week. My new goal is to represent the United States in Rio de Janeiro as part of the

2016 Paralympics Table Tennis Team. Echoing in my head is Dad's softly spoken assurance: "You can do that."

But of course I can. Why not?

APPENDIX

Coroner's Investigation

Name of Deceased: Helen Margaret Hall
Age: 39
Address: 1010 Grandview, Fullerton, California
Sex: Female
Place of Death: 109 N. Berkeley, Fullerton, California
Date of Death: September 4, 1957
Certificate Issued: September 5, 1957
Autopsy: Yes
Date: September 5, 1957
Cause of Death: Acute hepatic failure. Due to cirrhosis (portal) liver
Mortuary: McCormick Chapel, California
Married: X Single: Divorced: Widowed:
Relatives: Husband: Robert Hall
Place of Birth: Wooster, Ohio

REMARKS

Call received at 12:05 PM on Sept. 4, 1957 by Deputy Coroner R.W. Shoemake from Orange County Sheriff's Office (Station #90) via radio to Car 133, stating the Coroner's services were needed at 109 N. Berkeley in Fullerton.

Upon arrival at the above address, this deputy was met by Officers Richard Ray and Pearson of the Fullerton Police Department and was escorted into the bedroom where an examination of the remains disclosed a white female of the approximate age of 35 years, lying in bed on her left side and covered with a blanket; further examination showed the body to be in a relaxed position with the left hand to the mouth and there were blood spots on the bed sheet. A bottle of non-prescriptive sleeping tablets were on the dressing table at the left side of the bed.

Upon investigation, the father of the deceased, W.J. McGarvey of the aforementioned address, stated that his daughter, the deceased, had come to visit him the previous evening, bringing with her three daughters; that the same evening she had not felt well and had retired early; that throughout the night they could hear her getting up, going to the bathroom and vomiting; that the oldest daughter, Cynthia Louise had slept with her mother and the following morning, believing that the deceased was still ill and sleeping they had allowed her to remain in bed until approximately 10:00 AM, when the father of deceased had gone into the bedroom to awaken her; that he had found her cold and unresponsive to his attempts to arouse her and that he had then called Dr. Wickett, the deceased's personal physician; that he had been unable to contact Dr. Wickett since he was out of town and that he had then contacted the Fullerton Police Department who had, in turn, notified the Coroner's office.

A further statement from the father of deceased indicated that the deceased had been involved in an automobile accident approximately two years ago when she had been thrown from the vehicle and that about a year ago, while deceased and her husband had been on their way to Laguna to a tennis match, that deceased had a spell where she had stiffened up and her eyes had rolled back in her head; that, believing her to be dead, her husband had driven to Scripps Hospital in La Jolla where she was admitted, but that she had recovered. Mr. McGarvey also advised that the decedent had had vomiting spells for the past year but that he believed it was brought on by her nervous condition and that the deceased had always suffered with a back condition. It was also learned from the father of deceased that she had had no physical checkup since her admittance to Scripps a year ago; it was further determined that the blood spots on the bed sheet were due to deceased menstrual period. Since contact with Dr. Wickett was not possible due to his absence from the city, this deputy contacted Dr. Wilson, his medical partner who stated that he believed the deceased could possibly have had a tumor of the brain from the report received from Scripps and he also stated that the deceased was a "silent drinker".

Removal of the remains was made to McCormick's Mortuary at the request of the family and since no cause of death could be determined, it was requested of the Coroner's physician, Dr. Ray A. Brendt, that an autopsy be performed with results as shown above.

The Coroner, after reviewing this report, finding no evidence of foul play or violence, signs the death certificate using the Coroner's Physician's diagnosis as to cause.

Signed: E.R. Abbey, Coroner, Orange County
By R.W. Shoemake, Deputy
No. 9703
Dated: September 5, 1957

AUTOPSY RECORD
Coroner's Office
Orange County, California

Name: Helen Margaret Hall
Address: 1010 Grandview, Fullerton, California
Place of Death: 109 North Berkeley, Fullerton, California
Age: 39
Sex: Female
Race: Caucasian
Time of Death: September 4, 1957 at 7:00 A.M.
Autopsy witnesses present: A. Friend
Remains delivered to: McCormick Mortuary, Fullerton, California, September 5, 1957 at 12:30 p.m.

Height: 5'5"
Weight: 110 lbs.
Hair: Brown
Nourished: Slender
Muscle Development: Slender

Abnormalities or Identifying Marks
Wounds and other Injuries

Internal Examination: Upon opening the chest cavity the lungs are found to be fully expanded and somewhat heavy in weight. Both pleural cavities contain approximately 50 cc. of clear amber fluid. On sectioning the pulmonary tissue a severe edema with a moderately severe congestion throughout is noted. The tracheobronchial tree shows a slight amount of frothy mucus present in its most distal portion. There is no thrombo-embolic phenomenon present in the pulmonary vascular system. The pericardial sac is opened and contains approximately 10 cc. of clear amber fluid. The heart is of average size. The cardiac valves, chambers and musculature are not remarkable. The coronary artery system is examined and found to be patent throughout with no evidence of either recent or old obstruction. There is no sclerosis present.

In the abdomen the liver is one and one-half times as large as the normal expected size. The liver tissue is yellowish tan in color and on section shows moderate fibrosis throughout. There is a complete loss of normal liver structure and the capsule is slightly irregular. The gallbladder is distended with thin viscous bile and contains no calculi. The stomach is small and when opened contains a small quantity of brownish black liquid resembling fecal material. The remainder of the gastro-intestinal tract is not remarkable with the exception of the absence of solid particles of digested food. The pelvic organs, namely the uterus and ovaries, are not remarkable. The peritoneal cavity contains approximately 300 cc. of clear amber fluid. The pancreas, suprarenal glands, and kidneys are not remarkable.

Upon opening the head and reflexion of the scalp there is no evidence of recent or old injury. With the skullcap removed the brain is noted to be moderately edematous throughout. The cerebrospinal fluid is clear and appears to be under no increase in pressure. There is a slight increase in the diameter of the subarachnoid vessels in the mid-parietal and mid-occipital areas of the brain. In the most superior portion of the left parietal area of the brain there is a slight flattening of the convolutions with a minimal depression in this area. On section of the brain there is no pathology present except a mild congestion throughout. There is no tumor or fracture noted.

CERTIFICATE OF DEATH

DECEDENT PERSONAL DATA
NAME: Helen Margaret Hall
DATE OF DEATH: September 4, 1957; 7:00 A.M.
SEX: Female
COLOR OR RACE: White
MARITAL STATUS: Married
DATE OF BIRTH: June 18, 1918
AGE: 39
USUAL OCCUPATION: Housewife
KIND OF BUSINESS OR INDUSTRY: Own Home
BIRTHPLACE: Wooster, Ohio
CITIZEN OF WHAT COUNTRY: USA
NAME AND BIRTHPLACE OF FATHER: William J. McGarvey, Sr.—Ohio
MAIDEN NAME AND BIRTHPLACE OF MOTHER: L. Helen Donaldson—Penn.
NAME OF PRESENT SPOUSE: Robert Hall
PLACE OF DEATH: Orange County, Fullerton
LENGTH OF STAY IN THIS CITY OR TOWN: One Day
FULL NAME OF HOSPITAL OR INSTITUTION: At Home
ADDRESS: 109 N. Berkeley Ave., Fullerton, California
LAST USUAL RESIDENCE: California, Orange County, Fullerton, 1010 Grandview
PHYSICIAN'S OR CORONER'S CERTIFICATION: Deputy Coroner (illegible)
ADDRESS: Santa Ana, California
DATE SIGNED: SEPTEMBER 5, 1957
BURIAL OR CREAMATION: Burial
DATE: Sept. 6, 1957
CEMETARY: Loma Vista Cemetery
FUNERAL DIRECTOR: McCormick Chapel, Fullerton, California
CAUSE OF DEATH: Acute hepatic failure due to Cirrhosis (portal) of liver

ORANGE COUNTY SHERIFF'S OFFICE

CRIME LABORATORY

REPORT OF EVIDENCE EXAMINATION

CASE: DEATH

NO. 5884

DEFENDANT:

OTHER: Coroner

VICTIM: HALL, Helen M.

MATERIAL EXAMINED: BLOOD

OBSERVATIONS AND TESTS: A blood alcohol determination showed a level of .093%

CONCLUSIONS: An insignificant level of alcohol is present

EXAMINER: Ronald John Briglia, Assistant Criminalist

ABOUT THE AUTHOR

Cindy Hall, age ten

Cindy Hall Ranii studied Near Eastern Languages at the University of California, Berkeley and South Asian Regional Studies at the University of Pennsylvania. A retired educator with a doctorate in Educational Leadership from the University of Southern California she served as a teacher, principal, superintendent, and professor. She lives in Santa Cruz, California with her partner Shelly. They have four children and nine grandchildren.